RALLY
on the
HIGH GROUND

The National Park Service
Symposium on the Civil War

•

Ford's Theatre
May 8 and 9, 2000

Edited by
Robert K. Sutton

Eastern National
Serving America's National Parks
and Other Public Trusts

©2001 Eastern National

Eastern National provides quality educational products and services to America's national parks and other public trusts. Please visit our online bookstore at eParks.com

ISBN 1-888213-72-8

Edited by Robert K. Sutton
Designed by Jason M. Scarpello and Kristine Acevedo
Printed in the USA

FOREWORD

In the 2000 Department of the Interior appropriations bill, Congressman Jesse Jackson, Jr. inserted the language that brings us together. The language is brief and, I think, suggestive of possibilities. It simply says that Civil War battle sites are, "often not placed in the proper historical context." With that language, Congress directed the National Park Service to compile a report on the status of our interpretation of battlefield sites throughout the system. Then the language directed me, the Secretary, "to encourage Civil War battle sites to recognize and include in all of their public displays and multimedia educational presentations the unique role that the institution of slavery played in causing the Civil War." The Park Service—faithful to that mandate—has now compiled that report. It is a good report. It is quite candid. It consists of responses to a questionnaire that was sent to all of the managers of battlefield units and those answers bear reflection.

What I understand from those reports is that the National Park Service is doing a uniformly splendid job of presenting the facts of the battles themselves, often in immense detail, which in turn reflects the thirst and interest that visitors have for learning about what happened on those sites. They try to help us understand what Sir John Keegan refers to in his writings as the "mist of battle." The reports, I think, are equally candid in documenting our deficiencies in placing these battles in the larger context of both the causes of the war and the consequences—most notably—the issue of African slavery and its woeful legacy of racism and discrimination, which continues to this day.

As we undertake this task, I would suggest that there are a lot of reference points where we can see the National Park Service already pointing the way in their interpretation and context of other sites in the system. I am going to give you three or four examples in hopes that it will inform our ability to look broadly at these issues. One that comes to mind is Harpers Ferry, West Virginia, a remarkable town, that has been such a prominent site in American history. The Park Service, with the assistance of the Museum of the Confederacy in Richmond, is mounting an exhibit commemorating and interpreting the 200th anniversary of the birth of John Brown. Now, that is a remarkable initiative. Whether you consider John Brown to be a visionary and martyr, or whether you consider him an outlaw and a fanatic, or all of the above, there is no question that the raid on Harpers Ferry and subsequent trial and hanging of John Brown stirred and divided this nation as few events have before or since in our entire history.

I would also like to take you to the Boston African American Historical Site. It is a site that the Park Service is particularly proud of because it interprets a trail that includes a number of sites linked in history, including the African American meeting house where visitors can trace the rise and the development of the leadership role of African Americans in the abolition movement. It is for many visitors climaxed with the Saint-Gaudens sculpture on the Boston Commons commemorating the African American 54th Massachusetts Regiment, the subject of the movie *Glory*.

In the last couple of years, the Park Service has put together a kind of a new concept, authorized by Congress, called the Underground Railroad Park. It is different because it is a virtual park. It does not consist of any one place, it is about an entire movement, a network across much of the country. It gives the Park Service the opportunity to explain and honor the incredible network of people—North and South, black and white—who reacted to the fugitive slave law by organizing safe houses, assistance, communicating and assisting refugees as they moved up through the border states toward secure havens in Canada. It provides a marvelous opportunity to talk about the positive side of this long and continuing struggle toward a more perfect justice, with participation of many Americans from different regions of the country, black and white together.

Here in the District of Columbia, Bob Stanton, the Director of the National Park Service, has made a personal project out of showcasing the life of Frederick Douglass. His words continue to have extraordinary relevance for all of us today, and his home in the district honors this most effective and eloquent of all of the abolitionist leaders.

But the fact remains that it is the battlefields themselves that will always be at the heart of our remembrance of the Civil War. In each generation, Americans visit these sacred fields to locate their ancestors. They learn the strategy and tactics that gave birth to modern warfare. They find inspiration in the suffering and heroism of the participants and enrich their understanding of who we are as Americans. These places have remarkable meaning to our visitors. William Faulkner reminded us that "the past is not dead; it is not even past."

I want to emphasize that this Congressional directive is not meant in any way to compromise our successful and popular battlefield programs. What this Congressional mandate is about is challenging to find a larger view, lifting our eyes up from the din of battle, and seeing if we can enter into the lives of the participants in order to comprehend and reflect upon the causes and consequences of that struggle.

We have other opportunities coming at us in the National Park Service to expand our interpretation as well. I would like to give you just one example that has come as a result of recent action in Congress, in hopes that as we focus on the central task of battlefields, we can think more broadly about what we can draw from this period in history. We can use it to inform our public about who we are and how we address the future, while at the same time doing a more productive job of dealing with the legacy of the institution of African slavery.

Last March, I had occasion to accompany the President on his trip to Selma, Alabama to commemorate the thirty-fifth anniversary of Bloody Sunday. Frankly, it was an emotional moment for me because I, along with Congressman Jackson's father and many other Americans, was in the streets of Selma during the March of 1965. I had not really had an opportunity to reflect on that event and I found myself—remarkably, 35 years later—as the Secretary of the Interior returning to commemorate that moment in history. I found myself in charge of interpreting an event, a historical event, in which I had actually participated. And of course, I had occasion to reflect on how that moment, those weeks in Selma, leading to Montgomery, leading to the passage of the Voting Rights Act of 1965, has so profoundly transformed the role of African Americans in the political life of our country. I listened to the President remind us, in the words of President Lyndon Johnson that "history and faith meet in a single time in a single place to shape a turning point in man's unending search for freedom."

Now a couple of years ago in 1997, Congress designated the march route as a national historical trail. It authorized the Park Service, the Department of Transportation, and the State of Alabama to come together once again to develop an interpretive plan for the site that together make up this moment in American history. And as I met and talked with the participants from 1965, visited the sites, talked to the current city council members of Selma, it occurred to me once again, we have a choice about how we will do business there. That is to say, are we going to interpret this event and leave it at that, or in the spirit of Congressman Jackson's language directed to battlefields, are we

BURIAL OF SOLDIERS AT FREDERICKSBURG.

❉

going to think of this a little bit differently and ask ourselves, what is the context of Bloody Sunday and those events in Selma?

Of course, it does not take long to recognize that a pathway from Selma that led forward through the Voting Rights Act also takes us backward to Appomattox Court House and to the events immediately following Appomattox when African Americans received the right to vote. They went to the polls in extraordinary numbers, elected black officials to county governments, to state legislatures, to state offices, to the House of Representatives, and to the United States Senate. Many of these figures are mostly forgotten, but, in their time, they were eloquent, productive leaders who in many states laid foundations for the first time for public education in their states. They were the leaders in anti-discrimination legislation, public housing accommodations, and social services. And, I thought to myself, this brief moment in history, unfortunately, came to a halt within one generation, when African Americans again were turned away from the polls and denied the right to vote. It was there, in those events, that the pathway to Selma began, on which for a hundred years, church leaders, ministers, and public officials took the path toward Selma to reclaim the rights that had for one brief moment flowered in a period of American history, but now, were largely forgotten.

This is the task that Secretary of Transportation Rodney Slater, the Governor of Alabama, local officials in Selma, and I have decided to take up in the spirit of the broader implications of our history. We will be meeting in Selma to see if we can come together in a way that will interpret all of this history, for important reasons, because, without this context, it is impossible to really understand where we are, much less where we are going. Unless we understand where we have been—and that, of course, is the role of history and the challenge that is before us, because in each generation, we inform history with the values and insights of our generation—the task of history is never done. It is not just history, it is a living reality that is about our lives and how it is we work together, to inform and make our future better by understanding the past.

Bruce Babbitt
Secretary of the Interior
Winter, 2000

CONTENTS

INTRODUCTION

by Robert K. Sutton

On the morning of September 19, 1889, General William Rosecrans left his room at the Read House hotel in Chattanooga, boarded the Chattanooga, Rome and Columbus Railroad, and rode out to a spot near where he had stood twenty-six years to the day earlier. He, no doubt, felt a sense of irony, for the spot was the battlefield of Chickamauga where he had suffered his most crushing defeat during the Civil War. The Battle of Chickamauga had effectively ended Rosecrans' military career. But today, "Old Rosy" was a hero. Today, he would address veterans from both sides of the conflict. "People shall come and visit," he said, "with the interest due to the greatness of the events which occurred on this battleground. It took great men to win that battle, but it takes greater men . . . to wipe away all the ill feeling which naturally flows out of such a contest."

The following day, Rosecrans would again be one of the guests of honor. He and former Confederate General John B. Gordon would again board the train and ride to Crawfish Springs, Georgia. When they arrived, they mounted full-blooded steeds and made a grand entry to join 12,000 people who had gathered for more speeches and a gigantic barbecue. These events were all part of a rolling tide of momentum that less than a year later would culminate in the creation of the Chickamauga and Chattanooga National Military Park. Veterans from both sides of the conflict supported the effort. And when Congress passed the legislation creating this first Civil War battlefield park, it fully recognized this joint Blue and Gray effort. These battlefields would be protected permanently "for historical and professional military study," so that students and visitors could learn about "some of the most remarkable maneuvers and most brilliant fighting in the war of the rebellion."

The healing process would continue, and reach its apex when, in July of 1913, many of the surviving veterans from both sides of the battle at Gettysburg tottered up and shook hands at the same place where they had tried to kill each other fifty years earlier. Over 50,000 people came together for this "Peace Jubilee." And, on July 4th, they listened to President Woodrow Wilson, as he made his own Gettysburg address. As Professor David Blight has described so well in his essay, there was much symbolism in Wilson's appearance at this event. He was the first southern president elected after the Civil War. His father had been an ardent Confederate sympathizer. President Wilson earlier was quoted as saying that the South had "absolutely nothing to apologize for," in regards to its secession from the Union. Not surprisingly, then, Wilson's speech focused on unity. He reflected on the valor of the men who fought, the reconciliation between both sides, and concluded that the Civil War could now be considered "the quarrel forgotten."

The theme of reconciliation and healing was the context in which the Civil War battlefields were set aside as sacred places. This was a very good thing. Throughout world history, most civil wars, especially those as bloody as ours, generally ended bitterly. So, the fact that these former combatants could come together in peace and friendship was truly amazing. But, this "quarrel forgotten" had its downside as well. In setting aside their differences and in symbolically joining hands over the wall at Gettysburg, most Americans had forgotten that the war was fought over slavery, and that slavery was abolished when the war was concluded. They also forgot that, in large measure, the war had ended when it did because over 220,000 African American soldiers—135,000 of them former slaves—had joined the Union cause. Professor Blight observes that there were no black veterans at Gettysburg in 1913. The only African Americans in attendance "were the laborers who built the tent city, who built and cleaned the latrines and dispersed blankets to the white veterans." So, the war was over, the nation was healing itself, but the country had defaulted on its down payment toward emancipating the former slaves.

Slavery was the central cause of the Civil War. Each of the distinguished scholars who have contributed to this volume agrees with this statement. They would further agree that slavery was not the only cause of the war, nor was slavery President Abraham Lincoln's stated cause at its beginning of the war. But, when all of the issues are reduced down to their essence, it is hard—if not impossible—to deny that the institution of slavery caused the Civil War. Many of the essays that follow cite Confederate Vice President Alexander H. Stephens' statement at the beginning of the conflict, on the relationship between the Confederate government and slavery. "The new constitution," Stephens declared on March 21, 1861, "has put to rest, forever, all the agitating questions relating to our peculiar institution—African slavery as it exists amongst us—the proper status of the Negro in our form of civilization. This is the immediate cause of the late rupture and present revolution." He left absolutely no doubt that the institution of slavery was the central pillar upon which the new government would stand.

What was the institution of slavery like? Professor Ira Berlin warns in his essay that it is a grave mistake to underestimate the complexity of slavery. But, Berlin continues, this complexity should not dissuade us from studying or explaining the "peculiar institution." He further provides a historical context to help facilitate our understanding. Slavery was the most vile, obscene, hideous fact of American history. It forced the separation of husbands from wives and parents from children. It brutalized people physically and psychologically. But, as Professor Berlin also points out, slaves did not surrender to their plight. Slaves carved out niches for family life, religious worship, education, formal and informal associations, and created a remarkable culture, language, music, and cuisine. They created these in secret. "Indeed," Professor Berlin says, "the creative legacy of slavery is so great that we must concede that if slavery is the darkest part of America's past, it may also be the most creative part of America's past."

Slavery was a profitable economic institution. Over the years, scholars have debated whether the slave economy was efficient or inefficient—that debate likely will continue. There is no doubt, however, that cotton, the major crop produced by slaves, was by far the most valuable export crop in the United States. Professor James Horton points out that by 1840, cotton was more remunerative as an export than all other exports combined. Not only was the fruit of their labor lucrative, but the laborers, themselves, were quite valuable as investments. Professor Eric Foner notes that by 1860, there was more capital invested in slaves than in all railroads, all factories, and all banks—North and South—combined. So, economically, the institution of slavery was profitable.

Furthermore, slavery was protected by the United States Constitution. Southern states held enough political power that it was impossible to expect that the Constitution would be amended to abolish slavery. Thus, enslaved and free African Americans, alike, increasingly recognized that a war was the only realistic hope to end this institution. So, as the southern states moved toward possible secession, most free blacks and slaves were cheering them on. Professor Horton quotes black abolitionist Charles Lenox Remond, whose advice to southern states was "stand not on ceremony, go at once."

When the South actually did secede, Horton observes, African Americans ignored the fact that President Lincoln's initial war aim was to reunite the Union and not to end slavery. They enthusiastically threw their full weight behind the Union war effort for as long as it took to kill the institution of slavery. At first, their offers to fight were not accepted, so they volunteered their services to do anything to help in the war effort. Professor Berlin observed that as more and more contraband slaves came into Union camps, Union soldiers increasingly recognized and sympathized with their plight and gave them aid and comfort, although the early official policy was to exclude fugitives from Union lines. Eventually the government changed its policy, allowing escaped slaves to be considered as contraband property of war. Technically they were not free, but rather confiscated property. For all intents and purposes though, as far as they were concerned they were no longer slaves.

Then, not long after the Emancipation Proclamation, black men were allowed to volunteer for military service. Eventually nearly a quarter-of-a-million black soldiers would participate. For them the stakes were very high. If they were captured, two things might happen to them—both bad—and both worse than what their white counterparts would face. In the better of these bad options, they would be sold into slavery. In the worst, they could suffer the fate of the black soldiers at Fort Pillow, Tennessee, and elsewhere, who surrendered and were then massacred, along with their white officers, by Confederate soldiers. But, if they were successful, they would help end slavery in the United States forever.

Slaves in the deep South, who could not escape to Union lines, found creative ways to sabotage the Confederate war effort. Professor Drew Faust has observed that the white women left to tend the plantations were ill equipped to manage the slaves left in their charge. For their part, slaves found new and creative ways to make their owners' lives miserable. Professor Faust quoted one Mississippi woman who said that she feared "the blacks more than [she] did the Yankees." In short, the entire institution of slavery was in chaos behind Confederate lines. Slaves did not rise in open rebellion, but they just as surely undermined the social fabric of the South and sped the destruction of slavery from within.

The reasons African American soldiers fought and the slaves still in bondage resisted their plight were clear—they wanted to end slavery. The motivations of white soldiers were more complicated. Professor James McPherson describes two reasons that soldiers fought. First, they fought for their comrades. They believed that carrying their personal weight in battle was very important. It was far better to take their chances in battle than for the people back home to hear that they were cowards. The soldiers also fought for causes. Ironically, both sides believed they were fighting for liberty. To most Confederate soldiers, liberty meant that they were exercising the principle of the American Revolution, to determine their form of government and to defend their homes, property, and families from the northern invaders. To the northerners, on the other hand, liberty was correlated with the republican ideal that this democratic form of government was based on majority rule. It had to survive. If it did not, in Lincoln's words, "the last best hope on earth" would be lost.

As the Civil War dragged on, Union troops increasingly accepted the abolition of slavery as a cause worth dying for. Professor McPherson cites Ohio Colonel Marcus Spiegel, who in 1863 wrote to his wife that he did not "want to fight for Lincoln's Negro population any longer." A year later, just before he was killed in Louisiana, Spiegel again wrote to his wife, but this time he had observed the "horrors of slavery," and he was now "a strong abolitionist." Many, many other northern soldiers shared Spiegel's change of heart.

Colonel Spiegel's letters to his wife tell how he felt about the war, but what about his wife? How did the war affect her? How did it register to all of those left behind? Professor Faust notes that the homefront was quite different for each side. Four out of five white southern men of military age entered the army, as compared to less than half of northern men. And, a much higher percentage of southern men died in comparison to the overall population—6% in the North and 18% in the South. As noted earlier, southern women who had to tend to plantations had the doubly difficult task of providing for their families and trying to manage the slaves, who could sense that their freedom was not far off. But all women in the region had a difficult time. With so many men gone, and a chronic shortage of food and other necessities, many families grew truly destitute. In general, the situation in the South for the families left behind was much more difficult than in the North. And, as if the want of necessities was not enough, many of these families had to contend with the devastation caused by battles that had been fought in their backyards.

Once the war was over, it became increasingly important to the soldiers on the losing side to understand and explain why they had lost. To General Robert E. Lee the reasons were not terribly complicated. As he bid farewell to his troops at Appomattox Court House on April 9, 1865, he simply noted that "after four years of arduous service, marked by unsurpassed courage and fortitude, the Army of Northern Virginia has been compelled to yield to overwhelming numbers and resources." The so-called "lost cause" theory thus was born. To elaborate on Lee's statement, this theory suggested that the Confederacy was doomed to defeat almost from the outset, because the North simply had too many men, too much industrial might, too much of nearly everything for the South ever to win the final victory. That rebel soldiers fought so bravely, that the southern people were so committed to the cause, and that the Confederate military had such capable leaders were the reasons that the war lasted as long as it did. But, when General Ulysses Grant threw thousands upon thousands of soldiers into battle in the last year of fighting, there was absolutely no chance for a Confederate victory.

Like a poorly fortified infantry line, the "lost cause" viewpoint had several weak points. Throughout history, a number of weaker opponents won stunning victories. In our own Revolutionary War, the struggling colonies faced enormous odds, lost more battles than they won, and had to contend with the fact that nearly one-third of their own population supported and even fought for the enemy. Yet, the colonies eventually gained their independence.

While the Union victory was a simple proposition for Lee, historians since have recognized that the issues are a bit more complex. As the Civil War centennial approached, a number of scholars reevaluated the various Union victory theories as retrospective studies. Among these works, David Donald edited a small volume, titled *Why The North Won the Civil War* (1960). Five leading American scholars from that period prepared papers from each of their specialized interests—economic, diplomatic, military, political, and social history—to analyze why the North won and the South lost. In this, the first "how and why" book on the war, each historian argued that the result owed less to the North's superiority in resources than to its more competent leadership, application of resources, and superior commitment to its mission.

Since 1960, several other "how and why" volumes have been published. The most recent, *Writing the Civil War* (1998), edited by James M. McPherson and William J. Cooper, Jr., surveys the most recent scholarship on the Civil War, focusing on military, political, social, economic, and constitutional issues. In this volume, the scholars again analyzed the "lost cause" interpretation. Not only was this theory fraught with serious problems, it was, in fact,an incorrect theory. Northern victory, instead, resulted from an evolutionary process, in which the iradication of slavery became a political and military goal, along with the destruction of other Confederate civilian property. Further, when Grant became overall commander of Union forces, he recognized that he operated under a civilian commander-in-chief, and he balanced military strategy with political realities to concentrate his military strength in ways that would achieve ultimate victory. On the other hand, the Confederates were not able to establish the same overall military purpose. Recent scholarship also strongly suggests that the South essentially lost its will to fight toward the end of the war. Another trump card, often overlooked in earlier studies, was the addition of over 220,000 African American soldiers at a critical point in the war, which helped to seal Union victory.

But, what does the Civil War mean for us today? Dwight Pitcaithley, chief historian for the National Park Service, has posed this question as the "so what" of the Civil War. Abraham Lincoln predicted in his Gettysburg Address that the Civil War would usher in a "new birth of freedom." And freedom, as Professor Eric Foner says, "is the central word in our political vocabulary." No word has been invoked more frequently. Further, the meaning of freedom has not been fixed, and has changed frequently throughout our history. The Civil War dramatically expanded the definition of freedom. The Thirteenth, Fourteenth, and Fifteenth amendments to the Constitution, ended slavery then after the war forever. All citizens—whether they were previously free or enslaved—now had equal protection under the law, and all males had the right to vote. During Reconstruction, these revolutionary ideals were put into practice. African Americans voted and held political offices. After Reconstruction, the nation retreated from its commitment to liberty and found ways to deny these blessings of liberty. This retrenchment, however, was not permanent. Future generations would determine that the Civil War amendments were indeed intended to do exactly what they said.

So, the "new birth of freedom" was a legacy—one of the "so whats"—of the Civil War. Civil War battlefields are another legacy. The paradigm under which the Civil War battlefields were created was healing, reconciliation, and remembrance in addition to the fighting that took place there. As Professor Edward Linenthal points out, however, sometimes this remembrance went to extremes. At Harpers Ferry National Historical Park there is a monument to a gentleman named Heyward Shepherd. Heyward Shepherd was a free African American resident of the town, who, in one tragic twist of fate, became the first casualty of John Brown's raid in Harpers Ferry. In 1931, the United Daughters of the Confederacy erected a monument to Shepherd's memory, not as someone tragically caught in the crossfire, but as a faithful black who refused to join the abolitionist forces. The monument extols the virtues of slavery, although Heyward was not a slave, and tried to demonstrate that the whites really knew what was best for blacks before the Civil War. Pearl Tatten, an African American music director at Storer College in Harpers Ferry attended the dedication for the Shepherd Monument. She stood up during the ceremony and said that it was wrong to dwell on the slave past, but instead she wanted to push "toward a larger freedom not in the spirit of the black mammies but in the spirit of new freedom and rising youth."

Professor Linenthal points out that National Park Service staff, after great soul searching about whether or not the monument should even be in the park, decided that the Heyward Shepherd Monument should remain, and that an interpretive marker should be placed nearby to explain its interesting history. Park management was attacked from all sides. Members of the NAACP wanted the monument destroyed, and neo-Confederates accused the park of catering to political correctness. So, instead of avoiding controversy, park management steadfastly held its ground. As a result, visitors now can see the big picture, the United Daughters of the Confederacy text on the monument and the park interpretive marker, which discusses the controversial issues. Both messages are instructive and important in the evolution of Civil War interpretation.

The symbolism surrounding Heyward Shepherd, of course, is much larger than the monument and the interpretive plaque. John Brown brought his little guerrilla army into Harpers Ferry with the intention of capturing the government arsenal there, then distributing the guns to slaves and free blacks to start a rebellion to end slavery. Although John Brown's raid was a dismal failure, and although Mr. Shepherd was in the wrong place at the wrong time, the event itself became a catalyst for the Civil War. So, in this context, this story has the potential to enter a much larger interpretive arena.

Congressman Jesse Jackson, Jr. recognized that this large palette, like the Heyward Shepherd/John Brown story, offered the setting for a new paradigm of National Park Service Civil War interpretation. As he wrote the report language for the 2000 National Park Service appropriations bill, encouraging park managers to enrich their interpretation, he envisioned that battlefields could become classrooms to explain how this cataclysmic event influenced American history and culture. And the lens through which he viewed these events was the metaphor of an earthquake, which goes something like this: Jackson defines the period from 1619, when the first slaves arrived on

American shores, until 1861, as the "tremor" phase. The constitution was written, protecting the institution of slavery, and Congress frequently compromised to accommodate slavery. The period from 1861 to 1865 was the great quake phase, the American Civil War. Then, everything from 1865 to the present has been the "aftershock" period. Some of these post-Civil War tremors have been intense, and have forced us to reflect on our history. But the Civil War perfectly exemplifies this metaphor. It shook the nation like no other event. It redefined the concepts of liberty and freedom. But it did not end racism, it did not end hatred, and it did not establish racial equality.

National Park Service Civil War battlefields certainly will not right all the wrongs of the past. But, they have the opportunity to become laboratories, places that will help all Americans, from all ethnic backgrounds, understand their past. People should expect to visit a Civil War battlefield and come away with an understanding of not only who shot whom, how, and where, but why they were shooting at one another in the first place. And, when the story of the shooting is finished, visitors should understand that all of this bloodshed turned the nation in a different direction. The Civil War reshaped the national economy, the political system, and the social structures in ways that still reverberate in our local and national lives today. The essays that follow are written by many of our most eminent scholars on the Civil War period. They will serve as a primer to help develop a new paradigm for interpreting our Civil War battlefields.

A MORE PERFECT UNION

by Jesse L. Jackson, Jr.

Congressman Jesse L. Jackson, Jr. began his service in the United States House of Representatives on December 12, 1995. He was sworn in as a member of the 104th Congress—the 91st African American to be elected to Congress. He was born in the midst of the voting rights struggle on March 11, 1965, and spent his 21st birthday in jail in Washington, D.C. for taking part in a protest against apartheid in South Africa. During the fall of 1997, Congressman Jackson and his staff toured many of America's Civil War battlefields, and observed, first-hand, how the National Park Service presents the story of the Civil War. From that experience, he introduced report language into the National Park Service appropriation budget that encouraged National Park Service Civil War park superintendents to expand the scope of their interpretation to include the discussion of such topics as slavery.

Introduced by Robert G. Stanton
Director of the National Park Service

Today, I want to share with you some of my life and speak to you out of my experience. While I hope to be intellectually sound and reflect accurate information, I rely on academics for much of my information, many of whom, like Dr. James McPherson and Dr. Eric Foner, I respect to the utmost. I am not a historian and I am not an academic. I am an activist and a practicing politician. I prefer to think of myself as a public servant but I am not naive about the profession I have chosen. I was not a history major in college. I did not know that much about the Civil War before coming to Congress. I visited my first Civil War battle site about three or four years ago. What I try to do is to reflect seriously on who I am, what is the context out of which I have come, and I also try to understand my surroundings and interpret them in a way that will better my community, even as it makes all Americans better.

Secretary of the Interior Bruce Babbitt shared the challenge of trying to interpret the significance of Selma, Alabama. Let me share with you my perspective on the importance of Selma. On Bloody Sunday, March 7, 1965, John Lewis, now Democrat from Georgia, 5th Congressional District, was beaten mercilessly for trying to cross the Edmund Pettus Bridge for that fundamental American right, the right to vote. I was born March 11, 1965, four days after the event known as Bloody Sunday. On Tuesday, March 9, 1965, the Reverend James Reeb, a white Unitarian minister from Boston, Massachusetts, was hit in the head with a baseball bat and knocked unconscious by a white man in a small group, who attacked him and two of his friends. My father, the Reverend Jesse Jackson, sought to assist African Americans in the right to vote and arrived from Chicago to join Dr. Martin Luther King, Jr. on March 10th, for that right. The very day that I was born on March 11, 1965, the Reverend James Reeb died, never recovering from a coma. My father, who had been run out of Selma, stopped at a pay phone, and called my mother in Greenville, South Carolina, where he found out I was born. He was so overwhelmed by the history of that moment that he almost named me Selma. Thank God for my mother's better judgment.

On Sunday, March 21, 1965, Dr. King began a fifty-seven-mile-long voting rights march from Selma to Montgomery, Alabama. On Thursday, March 25, 1965, the march arrived in Montgomery. While transporting a marcher back to Selma that evening, Mrs. Viola Liuzzo, an Italian-American housewife and a mother of five in Detroit, Michigan, was shot in the head and killed on Highway 80. On August 6th of that year, President Johnson signed the Voting Rights Act of 1965 into law. I was, therefore, literally born in the middle of the voting rights struggle.

What does that tell you? It tells me that the bread that my parents had cast upon the water thirty-five years ago came back in the form of the ninety-first African American ever elected to Congress, out of a total of approximately 11,500 Americans who have served in the Congress of the United States. If this were a Baptist church this morning, I would tell you that is another way of saying that the seeds that my parents planted in the struggle for the right to vote came back in the form of elected fruit. It is another way of saying that the prayers that my grandmother prayed—keeping me safe for my graduation, for my success—were the substance of things hoped for. Because in her life—she was eighty-five years of age when she died—she never had the opportunity or the right to an education in America. She knew that her parents were slaves. She prayed that one day her prodigy in the next generation, might, like many of us, pray that our children would have a better opportunity to grow, to develop, to earn, and indeed to be granted our full citizenship rights. That is another way of saying that "faith is the substance of things hoped for, the evidence of things not seen."

My experience in Congress has been quite a diverse one. I learned very early on that politics in Congress has a lot less to do with Democrats and Republicans, left or right, liberal or conservative, and a lot more to do with North and South. When I first arrived in Congress, I sought a seat on the House Transportation Committee. There were three available seats on that occasion. A conservative member from my state, knowing that I wanted to provide economic opportunity and growth for my congressional district, fought very hard—even though we are in the same party—to keep me off that committee. He feared that if my district grew economically, that growth might have some kind of adverse impact on his district. And so, the very first fight that I confronted in the Untied States Congress was my liberalness versus his conservativeness, even though we were in the same political party. I thought we were going in the same direction. Shortly thereafter, I focused my attention on joining the House Appropriations Committee and other Democrats initially sought not to appoint me. Because Democrats have been losing seats in the South, those marginal Democrats, who essentially could be conservative Republicans, needed to be on strong committees in the United States Congress, so they could go back and tell their constituents that they were necessary to the Democratic agenda.

So, even though I had been in Congress longer than some members, they were appointed to the House Appropriations Committee over me because there was a compromise, if you will, to ensure they would have better electoral opportunities. I observed the voting patterns of members of Congress, many of whom vote more regionally and locally for their districts, rather than doing the party's business. I listened very carefully to the rhetoric, not only of Democrats but also of Republicans. And I wanted to know more about the underlying currents of this North-South political dynamic. I went on three different tours of Civil War sites in the eastern theater. Some of you knew at the time that I was a member of Congress, others did not. As I sought and probed answers to very difficult questions from some members of the National Park Service, many of those who did not know I was a member of Congress, informed me that in order to change their opinion about what they saw and did, it would take nothing less than an act of Congress.

So, less than one session later, I have given those folks their act of Congress. Now let me try to tell you my perspective once again. This time with the force of the law.

One point that I want to make is that while 11,000,000 people visit National Park Service Civil War sites, most Americans never get the opportunity. Either they do not have the time or the financial wherewithal to do what I did. I traveled to more than twenty sites throughout the country. Most Americans go to one site. Of the eleven million visitors, most of them are raised around one site, and, therefore, they never understand the sweep of events from Harpers Ferry through Appomattox Court House. One of our challenges was to ensure that if an American visited one site he or she would develop a full appreciation of the whole war. It is quite possible that one could visit, for example, the site at Appomattox and never hear the name John Brown or know anything about any of the other battles. And that, quite frankly, is a very limited and very narrow interpretation of that single site. Obviously, coming from the home which I came from, I understood that race was a problem in America. But only my experience in Congress, at the Civil War battle sites, and through my reading and thought, took me to a new level of seeing the depth and the breadth of the problem. I discovered during this period that race is the most central factor in American history. Race, I must tell you, is the lens through which I, as an African American, view American history.

Let me break it down into its three phases. I use the metaphor of an earthquake. Phase I—from 1619 to 1861—I refer to as the "tremor" phase of our nation's history. It is during that period that the Constitution of the United States was written. It is during that period that many states were created, predating the formation of the federal government. It is during that period that the racial compromises were instituted, of admitting one free state and one slave state into the Union to keep the balance of power in Congress, so that the federal government might have a fair chance of surviving. During part of this period, the Gag Rule was enacted, meaning that the issue of slavery and race was not to be discussed in the Congress at all. Thomas Jefferson observed during this period that: "When I think about the institution of slavery on the one hand and I think about God being a just God on the other, I shudder for my country." He felt what I felt.

Phase II I refer to as the "great quake" phase—from 1861 to 1865—the events that we have come now to know and appreciate as the American Civil War. Everything from 1865 to the present is Phase III, or what I call the "aftershock" period, forcing every generation to reflect upon the magnitude of the quake that almost cost us the nation. Racism or states rights, that is, states rights as a cover for racism, is a major reason prohibiting us from building a more perfect union. I like to use this particular metaphor—the earthquake example—because it is more instructive for defining the nature and scope of the problem than any other paradigm. Whatever you feel about Democrats, Republicans, liberals, conservatives, moderates on economic issues, or liberals and conservatives on social issues, no period in history is greater in defining who we see ourselves as today as the Civil War. Most Americans do not fully appreciate that who we are today and what we have become today was in response to fundamental questions, in which race was central. Whatever you feel about the great quake, the Civil War, pro-Union or pro-Confederacy, it has left us with Democrats and Republicans, liberals, conservatives and moderates. Thus we have a new paradigm. All we can conclude from that event is that when it comes to fundamental rights for all Americans—even in the year 2000—that paradigm has been unable to help us fundamentally build a more perfect union. That political paradigm is incapable of advancing fundamental rights for all Americans. So, into the interior bill, I introduced language to put the battles in a particular context. "The Civil War battlefields," the language reads, "throughout the country hold great significance, and provide vital historic educational opportunities for millions of Americans. There is concern, however, about the isolated existence of these Civil War battle sites in that they are often not placed in the proper historical context.

"The Service, to all of your credit, does an outstanding job of documenting and describing the particular battle at any given site, but in the public displays and multimedia presentations, it does not always do a similar good job of documenting and describing the historical, social, economic, legal, cultural, and political forces and events that originally led to the war which eventually manifested themselves in specific battles. In particular, the Civil War battlefields are often weak or missing vital information about the role that the institution of slavery played in causing the American Civil War.

"The Secretary of the Interior is directed to encourage the National Park Service managers of Civil War battle sites to recognize and include in all of their public displays and multi-media educational presentations, the unique role that the institution of slavery played in causing the Civil War and its role, if any, at the individual battle sites. The Secretary is further directed to prepare a report to Congress on Dr. King's birthday, January 15, 2000, on the status of the educational information currently included at Civil War sites that are consistent with and reflect this concern."

I believe that each of these sites provide us with a way out of our historical dilemma. I must also acknowledge that only from the perspective of an African American do we view history through the lens of race. But in order to be effective in our nation, we cannot be obsessed with that vision. We must also be able to interpret for all the American people a way out of the crisis of which all of us are the beneficiaries. That can be accomplished through the language of the economy and by turning up the hearing aid by which all Americans hear all political dialogue. I believe in the year 2000 that it is clear that the crisis will be resolved only when every American is provided with economic security—employment, health care, education, and housing. From the African Americans' perspective, it would be perceived and considered a down payment on reparations, but that won't end racism. It does, however, give us the best chance of dealing with it. So how do we rise above liberalism and conservatism to build the progressive coalition we need to build a more perfect union?

Dr. James McPherson said that nearly all the first ten amendments to the Constitution apply the phrase "shall not" to the federal government. In fact, eleven of the first twelve amendments place limitations on the power of the national government. However, beginning with the Thirteenth Amendment in 1865, six of the next seven amendments radically expanded the power of the federal government at the expense of the states. Every one of them grants significant new powers to the government with the phrase "Congress shall have the power to enforce this article." We need to revive this tradition of positive amendments, which is what I propose to do.

Not long ago I proposed an amendment to the Constitution of the United States granting every American the right to an education of equal high quality. Not long ago, my father was in Decatur, Illinois. He was there to assist a group of students who were expelled from a local high school for two years for a fight they were alleged to have engaged in. When they filed a federal lawsuit, the federal judge in that particular case said in his holding that while the Reverend Jesse Jackson and the students had a very legitimate argument, in the final analysis he had to rely upon the Constitution of the United States in making his final determination. What he said—and I think this is very instructive as part of the lens that I have shared with you—is there is no constitutional right in America to an education. No constitutional right. I thought long and hard about that and I thought about the struggle to achieve an education in this nation for every American, including my grandmother who prayed that one day I might have the opportunity to serve. It occurred to me that there is nothing more fundamental in our nation than the right to an education. But why wouldn't all Americans agree that every American should have a constitutional right to an education?

My premise is that not all Americans can agree that every American should have the right to an education, unless, when they visit, for example, these battle sites, something about the interpretation makes the right to an education for all Americans part of the unfinished business of what occurred there. If we do not conclude that from these sites, then everything else becomes political and tactical. We just support one side versus the other side. But if there would be the right to an education of equal high quality we would no longer argue for vouchers. We would be arguing about a more competitive public school system where all Americans could indeed grow and make a difference. It means that there would be more taxpayers in the future, because more Americans with a better education could make progress. But, if the state government is under no obligation to provide an equal education, or funds this side of the state differently than that side of the state, there is no constitutional remedy for this school system. Thus, we cannot make progress going into the future for all Americans.

This is a factor in building a more perfect union. Such an amendment is an outgrowth of these series of events. Neither Mr. Gore nor Mr. Bush will ever advocate the right to an education for all Americans. Why is that? Because the experience of men who have run for the presidency and are elected has never been the experience of being denied of an education. Most Americans who have had a quality education, including myself, would agree that the right to an education is a more fundamental right than the right to have a gun. Yet the right to have a gun is in the Constitution but the right to an education is not. I happen to think that the right to health care is a more fundamental right than the right to have a gun. The right to health care of equal high quality is not in the Constitution, but the right to have a gun is. I think that if given the choice today, more Americans would actually support the right to health care, rather than the right to a gun in their homes. Only with the appropriate interpretation of these historical events—of the Civil War Era—can those Americans ever arrive at the right to a more perfect union through health care, through education, and through housing. Americans have essentially concluded that they will never get the right to health care from Democrats and they will never get it from Republicans. Liberals will always want to spend too much, conservatives never want to spend enough, and moderates will not want to spend it long enough. That is the paradigm that the war has left us.

The war, and the end of slavery, left us with the unresolved question of "how do we educate all of these people?" Liberals said they were entitled to an education that everyone else was entitled to. Conservatives said no, they needed to pick themselves up by their own bootstraps. Moderates argued that they should be provided with an education for a limited period of time. Liberals argued that all races should live together; conservatives, that segregation forever was the best approach. They had the political power to enforce it, which led to Jim Crow, which was not overturned until *Brown vs. the Board of Education* in 1954.

In reaction to *Brown vs. the Board of Education*, conservatives from Virginia to Texas essentially closed down their public educational institutions, opening private schools for their children. Why did they do this? They did this because there was no constitutional basis for providing an education for everybody. By the year 2000, the cost of that private education has become so expensive, that now they argue that vouchers are necessary. This is an outgrowth of our unwillingness to deal with the fundamental issue that every American is entitled to an education of equal high quality, which, in turn, is an outgrowth of the Civil War legacy.

Now, with historical hindsight, we actually know more about the Civil War—its battles, troop movements, and commanders—than we do about many of the individual characters who played roles in the events themselves. Their memoirs and diaries are of extreme importance and historical significance. We generally know far more about the lives and deaths of Dr. Martin Luther King, Jr. and President John F. Kennedy, and the important personages of the 1960s than we do about the significant people of the 1860s. And so I want to offer a new paradigm, if I might. Here we stand in the year 2000. I represent a generation of Americans, black, white, Latino people of all colors and races in my congressional district, but I would like to think that I have influence beyond my congressional district. And almost everyone in this generation refers to what occurred in the 1960s as instructive for who they are. Dr. King, in the 1960s, looked not to himself for answers to the problem, he looked to the great quake—the Civil War period—for his response. In 1963, he stood in the shadow of the Lincoln Memorial and told Congress that it had issued some Americans "a bad check." It had "come back marked insufficient funds."

Over 135 years after the Civil War, the liberal, conservative, moderate paradigm has failed to provide every American with the security of justice. There is money for Kosovo, there is money for aid to foreign nations, but there is not enough money to invest in education for every American. Dr. King constantly referred to the Civil War period. From *Brown* in 1954, to the Civil Rights Act of 1964, to the Voting Rights Act of 1965, to the Open Housing Legislation of 1968, up until his assassination, this period is instructive and part of the aftershock phase of the nation's history. Those of us who have had historical hindsight stand here in 2000 and look back over the past thirty-five years and see that we have made progress. But in the year 2000, over 45,000,000 Americans still do not have basic health care, so the traditional liberal, conservative, moderate paradigm obviously has not worked.

Democrats today propose a patients' bill of rights, but that is only for people who have some form of health care already. Republicans want a medical savings account. You have to have a lot of money to have a medical savings account. So the number 45,000,000 is likely to grow to sixty to seventy million, unless they are given the fundamental right that the paradigm from the Civil War has failed to provide them. Therefore, with this historical interpretation, we then begin to arrive at the unfinished business of what is necessary from these events to build a more perfect union for all Americans. Let me close on one final example, because I am sure you have a number of questions.

Not long ago, three young white men dragged an African American man to his death in Texas. I saw African Americans and white Americans on television expressing their outrage over the significance of these events in 1998. They were horrible; I think all of us felt the same way. However, what I never heard from those events, was an interpretation that was helpful for us as a nation. But, I think I can share with you this new paradigm that might have made this event different. You have to dream with me for a moment. What the three white men and one African American had in common was that none of them had a college education. That is an economic issue. Remember now, the African American was hitchhiking. He needed a car. That is an economic issue. If there were lights on that road in Jasper, Texas on that occasion, it would have been a lot less dark. Lights on a road are an economic issue. Had there been more police on that road, it is quite likely that the African American might have survived the onslaught. That is an economic issue.

Imagine another world, where the three white gentleman and the one African American all had single family homes, were college educated and had children in college. In other words, they were kind of like us. Even though they may have had deep racial resentment, in the final analysis, they would have been less likely to act upon that resentment because they would have had options in their lives. A relative degree of economic security may not change racism, but it puts all Americans in the position where they are not as likely to act upon their racism. Imagine a world, like my world, where we have more to lose when we say or do something wrong. Imagine a world where those men, the three white men and the one African American had a college education, were all earning $50,000 or $60,000 a year, and had a college or graduate school education. While they may not feel very comfortable living together, fundamentally the situation might have been different because the options of their lives were dictating something else—opportunity. It has the effect of changing their behavior. What failed was that the nation's history got them there. Democrat, Republican, liberal, and conservative have not invested in all Americans as they have invested in some Americans' lives to get them there.

Here is another paradigm for consideration. Let us put the nation's heart on an EKG machine, and watch the wiggly line. The nation's heart continues to beat through the tremor phase of the nation's history. Then there is this great quake. Then everything is in aftershock from that point, including the death of John F. Kennedy, the death of Bobby Kennedy, the death of Martin Luther King, Jr. But imagine for a moment, that, God forbid, four presidents in a row were assassinated. We would consider that period of American history to be horrible, and a huge event on the nations' EKG machine. But even after the fourth assassination, the nation's EKG would not register as large an event as the Civil War. This would force us to reflect upon the actual nature of just how big the Civil War was, meaning that every generation must look back and see what had us so divided on fundamental issues. So, now maybe it makes sense that the Confederate flag debate in South Carolina, the Confederate flag debate in Mississippi, or George W. Bush speaking at Bob Jones University are such dividing issues.

What also makes sense is the conflict between the federal government and states' rights, which continues today at the highest levels of government. Al Gore said to the Congressional Black Caucus that the number one issue in 2000 is federalism. But when it came to Elian Gonzalez, he said it was a local issue and should have been handled in a state family court. Al Gore says he is going to appoint Supreme Court justices who support federalism if he is elected to the presidency. But when the rubber hit the road, he said he was not going to enforce federal law. Or, how about Microsoft? The statement from Microsoft said that, while it understood the federal remedy, it was most disappointed that the federal prosecutors and the federal appellate court did not look at how Microsoft wanted to handle it behind each individual state's laws, not relying upon that which seeks to build a more perfect union. Certainly Windows is sold in all fifty states in the Union, but Microsoft sought a remedy behind the fifty different states' laws. So central to the scope of being able to address these remedies, is this event—the Civil War. The idea that there was and is legitimacy found in the states' rights argument in that this case arose from this event—the idea that there is remedy found in conservative economic thinking, around states' rights.

Everyone in this room might say "I am not a racist," and I am not using race for the purpose of beating anyone over the head. Race simply provides us with an insight into America that helps us see where the nation is going in this phase of the nation's history. We have immigrants who come into the country now. But the problem is when immigrants come here they become Republicans who are liberal on economic issues but not on social issues, or Democrats who are liberal on social issues but moderate on economic issues. They all join the paradigm that is part of an outgrowth of these events, where the question of race is central to understanding it. I have been trying to build an airport in my congressional district because there are only about 11,000 jobs for the 600,000 constituents whom I represent. Therefore, I have about sixty people in my congressional district for every one job. On the other hand, Henry Hyde's district—in just one community in his district—there are 35,000 people and 100,000 jobs in that one community. So, they have three jobs for every one person. I want to build a third airport. I say to Mr. Bush and to Mr. Gore, let's get the FAA moving on doing a study for balanced economic growth and what an airport could do in our area. They say no, the local mayor is in charge of the FAA in Chicago. The problem with not building a new airport in my congressional district, however, has the broader effect of re-segregating the city of Chicago. Out by O'Hare Airport in the northwest suburbs, there are all whites—Democrats and Republicans—living near the economic opportunity; while on the south side of Chicago and the south suburbs that I represent, people are poorer and blacker. I am arguing for more social programs; my colleagues are arguing for more tax breaks. All are part of the dynamic that this event—the Civil War—created for contemporary American politics.

When I go to Vicksburg or Manassas, or any other battle site, I ask what is the historical significance of this particular site. The park service superintendent responds saying right here was a left oblique and right there was a right oblique. So, the historical significance of Vicksburg is about an oblique. After all that I have just shared with you, is the historical significance about military history or a military view of these sites? At these sites, nothing tells us that there were no more Federalists or Whigs, and the Democratic Party was split in two, North and South, because of slavery after Lincoln won, or that we ended up with a two party system, Democrats and Republicans, based on the legacy of slavery. Nor is there anything to say that Lincoln ran on a certain campaign platform, and that South Carolina and other southern states said that if he won they would leave the Union. Then, when Lincoln took office he said he would put eleven stars back on that flag. All that has more to do with the history of Vicksburg and Manassas than a left or a right oblique.

Better yet, if the history of Vicksburg is about obliques, maybe Congress should pass another bill eliminating the National Park Service Civil War battlefields and just turn them over to the Army. They can explain obliques better than you guys. The history of the site is not about an oblique. In fact, that is why the federal government is there, to offer an interpretation of the site that is broader than left and right obliques, or why Pickett decided to charge across the field into cannon fire. As Garry Wills has suggested in his marvelous book on the Gettysburg Address, the interpretation of Gettysburg battlefield has most to do with redefining the nation in the context of the Declaration of Independence rather than in the context of the Constitution. Both sides had found legitimacy in the imperfect Constitution. The southerners said they had a constitutional right not to be in the Union; northerners said the South did not have a constitutional right to leave. All used the Constitution as the basis for these arguments. So Lincoln, at Gettysburg, five months after the battle, said all people were created equal and endowed by their creator with certain rights. He did not rely upon that which was disagreed upon. He defined a new America from that moment forward. In fact, July 4, 1863 has more to do with the stripes on the flag than does July 4, 1776. So, because of the victories at Gettysburg and Vicksburg, the northern troops were able eventually to put the southern states' stars back on the flag. So on July 4th, when Americans are waving the American flag, they are celebrating—even though we have not told them yet—what occurred at Gettysburg.

Some people have said to me that we are losing some of our real estate and many of our Civil War battlefields to urban sprawl. Well, if the stories at these historical places are broadly interpreted and every American truly feels that the history represents them, there will be a much greater chance of saving these sites than talking about obliques. Let's look at Kennesaw Mountain as an example. It was a Confederate victory, or at least a Confederate slowing of the Union forces. It is maintained by the National Park Service and it draws about a million visitors a year. However, the City of Atlanta and its suburbs are sprawling. It might grow all the way out to Kennesaw Mountain. Well, if I were an African American mayor of Atlanta, or an African American politician, I would not care if it went all the way up Kennesaw Mountain and became a middle class African American community. However, if the story of Kennesaw Mountain were told in a broader interpretation, then even the African American who goes to Kennesaw can appreciate its historical significance. Then Atlanta would likely expand around but not up Kennesaw Mountain.

There would be no need for me to even get into the politics of what we know to be obvious, when one starts arguing whether or not this history is legitimate versus that history. But if the site is maintained by the government and has a broader interpretation where everyone finds their story and finds meaning in that site, the visitation will double or triple. But when I went to Kennesaw, they were only selling Confederate paraphernalia. They weren't even selling Union paraphernalia. Well, that can't possibly encourage a broader audience at the site. And, when I went inside, the story mentioned nothing else about the rest of the war, but just about Kennesaw Mountain and what happened there militarily. So Kennesaw isn't about the Civil War. If my children visit Kennesaw, and other American children visit Kennesaw, they should leave with more information than simply what happened there.

Some of us argue that the best historical recollection of a site is what a soldier from Pennsylvania or Tennessee had to say about it. So we go to the diary and interpret the battle and war from his point of view concerning what occurred at that particular site. That is the personalized interpretation of the site. Well, then, that's what happened at the site according to that one soldier and his or her interpretation. I understand that he was not fighting for slavery and that he did not own slaves. But, since we are interpreting for the whole nation a series of events, we can't just rely upon his interpretation of that event. So, if that is true, then my diary or the diary of somebody who served in Vietnam is what we should use to explain Vietnam. It had nothing to do with Kennedy, nothing to do with Johnson, nothing to do with domino theory, nothing to do with stopping communism. Instead it had something to do with the diary of the soldier who was in Vietnam who said he wanted a job and signed up with the military and ended up in Vietnam. Thus Vietnam is what he says about it. When we look through the history of Vietnam seriously, we look to what Kennedy had to say, we look to what Johnson had to say, we look to what Nixon had to say, we look to what the communists in Vietnam had to say about it. We then conclude we lost 58,000 American lives on this political mission. So, why is it when we go to the Civil War sites, we don't look to what Jefferson Davis had to say, or what Alexander Hamilton Stevens had to say, or what Lincoln had to say about it? Somehow we find comfort in elevating what the individual soldier had to say about it.

I hope that what I have shared with you today is something that is a broader based interpretation, that has great implications for saving and preserving the battle sites for all Americans. But it also has great implications for defining the future of what Americans should be fighting for and what they should be expecting from their federal government. There are those who are arguing in the Congress of the United States that these Park Service sites are better controlled under local flexibility and control. If they are successful, then all of you who work for the Park Service are coming back to Washington and we will find something else for you to do. However, if our efforts are successful, then these Park Service sites should be maintained in such a way that all Americans can feel the very nature of their story.

Today in our society, women still earn seventy cents to the dollar of what men make. Yet, they can't buy bread cheaper, they can't pay rent cheaper. From my perspective, we need to amend the structure of America to ensure that every woman has equal rights. That comes from that event. Forty-five million Americans still have no health care. Those Americans are not covered by any Democratic proposal or any Republican proposal, any liberal proposal or any conservative proposal or any moderate proposal. Those Americans were born here just like everybody else. They are entitled to the same rights under the Constitution, and that will only come from changing the structure of America, by guaranteeing that fundamental right. These rights come from that series of events called the Civil War.

Questions and Answers*

Question: As we are looking at interpretation in our Civil War battlefields and trying to do the best we can to expand what we do and make sure what we say is appealing to all Americans—not just the 11,000,000 who come to our battlefields—one of the criticisms that we receive is that if we start talking about things like slavery, we will diminish what we have done in the past—the right obliques and left obliques. What will happen is that our military history will be diminished and that is a great concern from a lot of our customers. Do you have a response to that?

Answer: Civil War history is probably the most written about subject in the world, because of its great implications not only for our nation but for other countries around the world. I guess my argument would be that there is no shortage of the military history of those events. We have the accounts of the individuals who participated in the events themselves. If you go to Gettysburg and a number of the sites around the country, you actually see physical markers of these events and there are sufficient diaries that have been written on that actual military history. As a matter of fact, one thing I can say without much equivocation is that there will not be much improvement upon what the actual people from their first-hand experience had to say about the military history of those events. So, there is a sufficient detailed history of these military events. There is not a sufficient detailed history of everything else that I have shared with you. And the absence of that history, I am suggesting, requires a certain lens to be able to see the implications of what occurred in those events with hindsight and what they have led us to in contemporary America.

Question: Would you support a similar provision to interpret the context for the Revolutionary War as well? This was a struggle that set forth the ideal—not realized—that all men are created equal?

Answer: I can't, on its face, see opposition to such instruction. However, I have not studied the Revolutionary War as I have put time and attention to this. So I would not want to make a commitment one way or the other without an understanding of those series of events that would be wor-

---

*In each session, questions were posed by the audience. The questions and answers (here and in each session) are included in full.

thy of something that would be instructive to the Park Service. So, whoever wrote the question, if you are willing to work with me on this and help broaden my understanding of that I would be more than willing to do whatever I could do to broaden my understanding.

Question: You never worked in a Civil War park, nor do you have experience in historical interpretation. You admit you are not a historian but a politician and an activist, in that you did not take an interest in the Civil War until four years ago. On the other hand, National Park Service historians in the audience have perhaps 2000 years in Civil War knowledge and experience. Given these facts why do you feel that you are qualified to impose your views of Civil War interpretation on the National Park Service?

Answer: I don't quite see my views as an imposition on the National Park Service, but consistent with what one of the directors of one of the sites shared with me—the will of the people, an act of Congress. So now that we have an act of Congress, that is the will of the people. At one level or another, the will of the people is at the site to interpret its broader implications and put it in historical context. That is much broader than left and right obliques. An act of Congress created the Department of the Interior and an act of Congress created the National Park Service. Furthermore, an act of Congress created your job and an act of Congress decided that local as well as state municipalities would not encroach upon this space because an act of Congress determined this space to be sacred. So, acts of Congress, long before I got to Congress, created these sites and made determinations about how these sites would be shaped to keep local governments and state governments from encroaching upon these sites. Acts of Congress also are responsible in one way or another for the interpretation.

I was in Andersonville. While it has great historical significance and holds a significant role in the history of nation, Andersonville is now the site of the National Prisoner of War Museum—through an act of Congress. However, if we want millions of visitors to learn anything about prisoners of war, why wouldn't we have the National Prisoner of War Museum in Washington where people come from all over the world to learn about national events of national significance? But an act of Congress, a political determination by the congressman of that district and the senator from that state, informed Lyndon Johnson that the history of Andersonville had great implications for that member of Congress and that senator's role in Washington and in advocating things for their state. So they didn't seek to change the history of Andersonville, they just simply sought to modify it by putting the National Prisoner of War Museum at that location. I happen to think that Andersonville has nothing to do with prisoners of war in Vietnam, has nothing to do with prisoners of war in Korea, and has nothing to do with prisoners of war in World War I or World War II, which the site now clearly explains and makes clear. Those events are central to the nation and are central to Washington, D.C. Andersonville is about—if you are talking about historical accuracy—what my colleagues in Congress want it to reflect.

I am not trying to do that at all. I am simply saying that through the nation's history, one inescapable issue is the issue of race. Moreover, it is a factor in every event from 1619 through and beyond even the impeachment of Bill Clinton. If those sites want to grow and be preserved for generations, they need to do a better job of interpreting these series of events and the role that they played.

SLAVERY IN AMERICAN LIFE: PAST, PRESENT, AND FUTURE

by Ira Berlin

Ira Berlin's most recent work, Many Thousands Gone: The First Two Centuries of Slavery in North America, *is already considered a classic work on American slavery. It was awarded the Bancroft Prize in 1999 as the best book in American history by Columbia University. In his book, Professor Berlin focuses on the first 200 years of slavery and finds that the interactions between the master and the slave were not as simple as often believed. Actually, the two shared a complex relationship in which the slave had considerable power. In addition to this work, Professor Berlin founded and served as the principal editor of the multi-volume* Freedom: A Documentary History of Emancipation, *and he has authored and edited a number of other works on slavery and freedom.*

Introduced by Frank Faragasso,
National Capital Parks-East

The ratification of the thirteenth Amendment to the Constitution in December of 1865 abolished slavery in the United States, formally, officially, and legally. Speaking soon after, a black preacher in the District of Columbia pronounced slavery to be "dead, dead, dead!" And it was. In the years that followed, southern planters and their allies proved extraordinarily resourceful in inventing new forms of labor extraction and racial oppression. But, try as they might, they could not reinstate chattel bondage. Yet, almost a century-and-a-half later, the question of slavery again roils the waters of American life. Indeed, the last years of the twentieth and the first year of the twenty-first century have witnessed an extraordinary popular engagement with the question of slavery. Slavery now has a greater presence in American life than anytime since December 1865.

This new interest in slavery has manifested itself in the enormous success on the big screen of the movies like *Glory, Amistad, Shadrach* and Oprah Winfrey's *Beloved.* They are followed on the small screen by the four-part TV series *African in America,* which traced the history of slavery in the United States from its very beginnings through emancipation. More recently, Henry Louis Gates took a sojourn to Africa where he confronted the painful matter of African complicity in the trans-Atlantic trade. These television docudramas parallel any number of radio broadcasts, including *Remembering Slavery: African Americans Talk About Their Personal Experiences of Slavery and Emancipation,* an audio-book collaboration between the Smithsonian Institution, the Library of Congress, and the University of Maryland.

These programs, in turn, come hard on the heels of John Michael Vlach's *Back of the Big House,* an exhibit at the Library of Congress. Presently, not too far from where we sit in Ford's Theater, workers are putting the finishing touches on the monument to black Civil War soldiers and sailors.

The memorial lists the names of some 200,000 African Americans, most of them former slaves. A monument to the *Amistad* stands in front of city hall in New Haven, and the *Amistad* itself has been reconstructed at Mystic Seaport. The UNESCO Slave Trade project is installing a string of similar shrines from Africa to the Antilles, which will be connected to larger sites of remembrance. In the United States, one such site, the multi-million dollar National Underground Railroad Freedom Center, is in the planning stages in Cincinnati. There are others and this, I should add, is just the beginning. In the last year of the twentieth century, according to the Gilder-Lehrman Center for the Study of Slavery, Resistance, and Abolition at Yale, some sixty scholarly books on slavery and related subjects have been published. To these any number of novels, children's books, chronologies, textbooks, and genealogies can be added. Slavery has been on the cover of *Time* and *Newsweek*. It has been above the fold in the *Washington Post* and the *New York Times*. And if all of that is not enough, there was the discovery of what we might term, Sally Heming's "blue dress."

Now Sally Heming's "blue dress" provides a reminder of how much slavery has become a part of contemporary politics. Bill Clinton recognized this early on, and hence the debate or kind of phantom debate over "The Apology," which Clinton eventually delivered at Goree, a former slave factory on the west coast of Africa. Actually, it was not quite clear what Clinton said at Goree, since the American media reported it so poorly, but it soon became evident that Clinton had indeed apologized because conservative congressmen demanded that he retract his apology. As the haze of dueling editorials over "The Apology" faded, the National Advisory Panel on Race Relations chaired by the distinguished historian John Hope Franklin hovered into view. Then the spotlight was stolen by disputes over the Confederate flag, which started in South Carolina, soon spread to Georgia, and then Mississippi.

Am I alone in seeming to think that every time you open the newspaper or listen to the evening news there is some new controversy on slavery? In Washington, it is the question of whether school children can visit an exhibit in a Baltimore museum with a euphonious name of "Great Blacks in Wax." In Richmond, it is the torching of Robert E. Lee's likeness on the River Walk, a local tourist attraction, that feeds the debate. Elsewhere similar events have similar effects, reminding us of almost the impossibility of escaping our slave past. In New York, there is a lawsuit against the Aetna Insurance Company for insuring slave property more than a century earlier. In Massachusetts, the Archbishop apologized for the Catholic Church's slowness on the question of abolition. In Washington, senators and congressmen discovered that slave labor built the White House and the Capitol. As these events resonate in the press, debates over thousands of schools named for Confederate generals, slave-holding politicians, including some of our most revered leaders in American history, are just beginning. Looming even larger is the vexed and troubled questions of reparations. Recently, Governor James Gilmore III of Virginia, a self-described history buff, tried to escape the implications of naming May as Confederate History Month by declaring that "the slavery issue began in Jamestown in 1619 and ended in Appomattox in 1865." Needless to say, Governor Gilmore was wrong on both accounts.

It is rare for Americans to engage their history, especially at this level of intensity and with this degree of persistence. As a people, the past has not been of great concern to us, and, particularly, this painful aspect of the past. So it is useful to ask the question, "why."

Surely part of the reason for this explosion of popular interest has something to do with the recognition of the sheer weight of slavery's importance. Simply put, American history cannot be understood without the institution of slavery. Slavery shaped the American nation, its economy, its politics, its culture, and its most fundamental principles. For most of American history, the mainland colonies and then the United States were a society of slaves and slaveholders. The American economy, of course, was founded upon the production of slave-grown crops. The great staples—tobacco, rice, sugar, and finally cotton—which slave owners sold on an international market, brought capital into the new colonies. That capital eventually funded an enormous economic infrastructure upon which the modern American economy rests.

CAMP BRIGHTWOOD, D.C. CONTRABANDS IN 2ND RHODE ISLAND CAMP.

❊

The great wealth that slaves produced allowed slaveholders to secure a central role in the establishment of the federal government in 1787. They quickly transformed that economic power into political power which they maintained between the founding of the republic and the Civil War. The majority of presidents, everyone from Washington, Jefferson, Madison, and Monroe to Jackson, Tyler, Polk, and Taylor were slaveholders and generally substantial slaveholders. The same was true for the Supreme Court, where a slaveholding majority was ruled successively by two slaveholding chief justices, John Marshall and Roger Taney, from 1800 to the Civil War. A similar pattern could be found in the Congress of the United States, and the control of Congress by politicians representing the free and the slave states was the central issue of antebellum politics. The power of this slaveholding class represented in the nation's leadership gave it a large hand in shaping American culture and the values that were associated with American society. It is not an accident that a slaveholder penned the founding statement of American nationality and that freedom became the central value in American ideology. Men and women who drove slaves understood the meaning of chattel bondage, as most certainly did the men and women who were legally defined as chattel. And if it is no accident that Thomas Jefferson wrote that "all men are created equal," then it is certainly no accident that the greatest spokesmen for that ideal from Richard Allen to Frederick Douglass and from W.E.B. DuBois to Martin Luther King, Jr., were former slaves and the descendants of slaves.

Slavery was also the central cause of the American Civil War, a war that more than a century later continues to stir deep emotions. This is properly so, for clothed in the rhetoric of biblical prophecy and national destiny, the American Civil War accompanied a profound social revolution. That revolution destroyed forever a way of life based upon the ownership of human beings. It restored to the former slaves proprietorship of their own persons. It liquidated, without compensation, billions of dollars of property, while forcibly substituting the relationship of free labor for that of slavery. Following that Civil War, the Constitution was amended to designate former slaves citizens, place citizenship for all Americans on new ground, and remove the disposition of these people beyond the jurisdiction of the states. In obliterating the sovereignty of the master over the slave, the Constitution handed a monopoly of sovereignty to a newly consolidated nation state, overturning that old regime in the South and setting the entire nation on a new course. The Civil War, in short, changed everything.

In the Civil War and the Reconstruction that followed can be found the main themes of nineteenth-century American history: state formation, political realignment, economic transformation, and class conflict. So too with the great ideals of American life: freedom, self-determination, the ability of individual men and women to shape their own destiny, drenched in the blood of some 600,000 men and women. No wonder the battlefields of American history, over which the National Park Service presides, are the sacred ground of the American people.

It would be comforting to conclude that the recognition of slavery's importance has driven the American people to the history books. I certainly would like to believe that the importance of slavery and the Civil War has brought us here today to integrate the history of slavery into the story of America's great national monuments and its sacred ground. However, there is more to it than that. There is a recognition, often backhanded and indirect, and sometimes subliminal or even subconscious, that America's largest and most pervasive social problem—what W.E.B. DuBois called the great problem of the twentieth century (and which is fast on its way to becoming the great problem of the twenty-first century)—that is, racism—was founded in the institution of slavery. There is a general, if inchoate, understanding that any attempt to address this question of race in the present must also address slavery in the past. And, indeed, this imperative is more compelling as the United States becomes a more racially segregated and a more unequal society. In short, behind this interest in slavery is a great crisis in the question of race.

It is precisely this confluence of the history of slavery and the politics of race, which suggest that slavery has become a language, a way to talk about race in a society in which black people and white people hardly talk at all except for perhaps the banter of sports or the groan of daytime television. In the language of slavery, black and white Americans have found a voice to address their deepest hurts, their greatest fears, and their festering anger at the all-too-depressing reality that so much of American life in the twenty-first century—access to jobs, access to housing, access to medical care, access to justice, even access to a taxi—is still controlled by the matter of race. The renaissance in the interest of slavery—the movies, docudramas, museum exhibits, monuments, living history exhibits, and books—have become a way, an emblem, a metaphor, and a sign of both the failure to appreciate and address directly the question of race and of the desire to do so. Part of the reason that we are here today is not only to appreciate the significance of slavery in the American past, but also to understand why it looms so large in the present. Perhaps more importantly, we meet to prepare our children for the burden they must bear as the descendants of a slave society. The subject of slavery on America's sacred grounds, its Civil War battlefields, speaks not simply to the question of the past, not simply to the question of the present, but ultimately to our posterity and the posterity of the Republic.

Gaining an appreciation of slavery's significance does not necessarily make it easier to address. Everywhere we find ourselves tripping over our historical and ideological shoelaces. Take, for example, the dispute over John Vlach's *Behind the Big House* exhibit, which was an exemplary presentation of slave housing by one of the nation's premier folklorists. Its placement in the Library of Congress angered the employees of the Library—mostly black, mostly non-professional—who demanded its removal. They saw the pictures of the slave quarters as a representation of the plantation metaphor that they had often employed in describing their own stormy relationship with the Library's administration. The Librarian of Congress, a historian by training and trade, quickly acceded to their demands. But no sooner was the exhibit dismantled, than the librarians at the Martin Luther King Memorial Library in Washington, D.C., welcomed it and made it the centerpiece of their Black History Month commemoration.

There was a similar kind of double take in the debate over "The Apology" for slavery, which began with great fanfare and ended with muffled silence. Likewise Governor Gilmore's attempt to balance the celebration of Black History Month with Confederate History Month in Virginia and the seeming inability of the white Jeffersons to come to terms with the black Jeffersons over access to the Monticello graveyard elicited the same quizzical response. These vexed cases, which appear regularly on the evening news, demonstrate how the discussion of slavery is not an easy one. While slavery may provide an entry point for a dialogue—the dialogue we so desperately need—on the question of race, it carries with it deep anger, resentment, indignation, and bitterness for some, along with embarrassment, humiliation, and shame for others. And here I speak of both black and white, for everyone is touched by this complex legacy of slavery.

Thus we create a selective history: The *Mayflower* is me, the slave ship *Brooks* is them; freedom fighters at Valley Forge is me, freedom fighters at Southampton is them; freedom is me, slavery is them. Even as we make slavery a surrogate for race, it becomes tangled in the old, familiar emotional briar patch. Discussions of slavery become muted by fears of embarrassment both personal and political, and this is not simply a matter of good manners. More than 130 years since slavery's demise, the question of slavery still sits on tender and sensitive grounds—so sensitive that some Americans cannot even say the word. For some it is "servants," or "servitude," a recognition of subordination but an obscuration of the slave's unique status as property. For others, it is "enslaved people" or perhaps more awkward still, "enslaved circumstance." Here is recognition of the slave's humanity and a pointed denial of the slave's consent to enslavement, but also a similar beclouding of the unique meaning of property in man. The struggles over nomenclature reveal that Americans—white and black—feel they need to address the question of slavery and understand it but don't know exactly how. The task of incorporating the history of slavery into the history of slavery's sacred ground, the task with which the National Park Service in Civil War battlefields have been charged, is complicated and confounding. It would be a great mistake to underestimate it, either in importance or difficulty.

What should the American people know about slavery? Obviously, there are many things. Some issues relate specifically to battlefields; some are more general. Let me initiate the discussion by making a few points. First, the story of slavery in the United States has two large and, in some ways, contradictory messages. Their contradictory nature is precisely what makes slavery such a difficult subject to appreciate. The first of those messages is that slavery is a physical and a psychological imposition, and that physical and psychological imposition stands at the heart of the history of slavery. The history of slavery in the United States is a hideous history of obscene violence, of mutilations, beatings, rapes, and murders, of the forcible separation of husbands and wives, and parents and children, of husbands forced to see wives abused, and of wives forced to do unspeakable things. It is the story of power over liberty; it is the story of a people victimized and a people brutalized.

But, there is a second theme for the story of slavery that is not the history of victimization and is not the history of brutalization. If slavery was violence and imposition, if slavery was death, slavery was also life. Former slaves did not surrender to the imposition, physical and psychological. On the narrowest of grounds, in the most difficult of circumstances, they created and sustained life in the form of family, churches, schools, and associations of all kinds. These organizations—clandestine and fugitive, fragile and unrecognized—created language and literature, history and aesthetics, as well as a philosophy expressed in story, music, dance, and cuisine. Slaves produced leaders and ideologies that continue to inform American life into the twenty-first century. Indeed, the creative legacy of slavery is so great that we must concede that if slavery is the darkest part of America's past, it may also be the most creative part of America's past. It is almost impossible to understand anything about American culture without understanding something about the creative legacy of slavery.

Thus, slavery cuts both ways. It is both a profound violation of our most fundamental ideals— ideals stated in our national charter. It is a nightmare from which we as a people have yet to escape. But slavery was also a period of great cultural creativity and reaffirmation of life. It was the story of heroic determination, not merely to survive but also to create lives worthy of the men and women who made them and then passed them on to their posterity.

How do we tell both stories? Let me put it differently. How do you of the National Park Service tell both stories? I think the answer is not easily. To tell the story of slavery merely in terms of captivity, violence and death, the destruction of families and the assault on culture is to tell only half the story. It leaves out the heroic struggle of men and women under extraordinary duress. If we do so, we can rightly be accused of denying the slave's humanity, and of denying the slave's ability to take control of part of their own lives and, indeed, to make their lives their own. On the other hand, to speak merely of the slave's agency and creativity is to deny the suffering that accompanied slavery, and to be rightly accused of idealizing and of romanticizing the institution. Put another way, how could things be so good if they were so bad? Or, if things are so bad, how could they be so good?

Much of the recent, excellent history of American slavery attempts to walk the fine line between these two themes. One way of avoiding the trap of telling one side or the other is to recognize that slavery was not a fixed relationship. It was a historical relationship. This means that the institution was always changing; that there is no one slave experience. Historicizing slavery helps us navigate between the history of slavery as victimization and death and the history of slavery as creativity and life. For slaves were constantly struggling with their owners, negotiating between those who had big power and those who had little power. It was precisely the struggle which allowed slaves to shape, and, upon rare occasion, control their lives and even to shape the lives of their owners and others in American society.

Such a perspective puts us in good stead when we turn to the primary task of the National Park Service—the interpretation of battlefields of the Civil War. For slavery stood at the heart of the conflict between North and South, the coming of the war, the war itself, and its ultimate outcome. These are large subjects. Certainly, there is a long tradition to the argument that slavery was not the cause of the war, but that the war's origins were in a sectional conflict that revolved around issues of economy: tariffs, railroads, and monetary policy. Others have employed the matter of constitutional principles, the rights of state and nation, while still others have focused on the failure of political judgment, bumbling politicians and fanatics who rejected a tradition of compromise. I believe all of these arguments are mistaken, not so much because there were not fanatics and bumblers—plenty of those; and not so much because constitutional principles were not significant—constitutional principles had enormous weight in antebellum America; not so much because economic interests did not have consequences—because they had enormous significance. All of those matters were important in the conflict between North and South. But, ultimately, they were all linked to the issue of slavery. Very few men and women stood for states' rights in the abstract. Many more understood states' rights as a means to promote or to protect their own cause. When Alexander Stephens, the Vice President of the Confederacy, declared that slavery was the cornerstone of his new nation, he knew whereof he spoke. And, certainly, slaves understood the significance of Stephens' truth.

It is precisely for that reason which makes it impossible to separate the history of America's sacred ground from the question of slavery. By appreciating the connections between war and freedom, we then can understand that slaves knew from the beginning that a Union victory was imperative for themselves and for their future. From the beginning of the war, slaves ignored the pronouncements of Republican politicians that the war was only to preserve the Union or that it was a white man's war, which had nothing to do with them. Slaves threw their full weight behind the federal cause, even when federal officials denied them a place. By the thousands, they volunteered their services as teamsters, stable hands, boatmen, butchers, bakers, cooks, nurses, orderlies, laundresses, or simple laborers. Hundreds of thousands of black men and women worked for the Union army. Ultimately, more than 135,000 slave men served as soldiers in the Union army, and others as sailors in the Union navy.

Deep in the Confederacy, where slaves were unable to escape to the federal lines and where black men were unable to enlist in the Union Army, black people did what they could to undermine the Confederacy and to strengthen the Union. By supporting the Union with their loyalty, with their labor, and with their lives, slaves provided crucial information, muscle, and blood for the federal war effort. No one was more responsible for transforming the war from a war for union to a war for freedom and, in the process, smashing their own shackles, than the slaves themselves. In short, to leave the subject of slavery out of the story we tell on our sacred grounds denies a large part of our history.

To be sure, slaves did not free themselves. Adding them to the history of the Civil War does not deny or diminish the part others played in the story. But it does, however, change the story. Take for example the case of "Billy Yank," historian Bell Irwin Wiley's name for the common Union soldier. Arriving in the South with little direct knowledge of slavery, tinged, perhaps, with an abiding contempt for black people, federal soldiers were greeted by slaves eager to test their owners' fulminations against Yankee abolitionists and black Republicans. Union soldiers soon found their camps inundated with slaves seeking sanctuary, offering to assist them in any way possible. In so doing, slaves took considerable risks. They not only faced sure punishment if they were captured, but they risked harm from Union soldiers themselves, who often turned on slaves violently. Still, some gained entry into federal encampments where they found work aplenty. The slave's labor cut to the heart of the soldier's military mission. Slaves were pleased to pass along information about Confederate troop movements, to assist in the construction of fortifications, and to guide Union troops through a strange countryside. Just as often, slaves ingratiated themselves to federal soldiers in ways that had no particular military significance. They forged for firewood, cooked food, and cleaned campsites, performing dozens of onerous jobs that otherwise would have fallen to the soldiers themselves. Northern soldiers did not have to be freesoilers, abolitionists, or even radical egalitarians to appreciate the value of the slave's services.

Soldiers were dismayed to discover that they had violated orders by harboring fugitives, many of whom had arrived in federal camps in tatters bearing marks of abuse. They grew increasingly angry when the men and women who cleaned their camps and cooked their food were dragged off to certain punishment by angry slaveholders. Indeed, even those soldiers who stoutly maintained that they fought only for Union bitterly resented being implicated in the punishment of men and women who had done nothing more than do them a good turn in exchange for a blanket or a few morsels of food. "I don't care a damn for the darkies," declared a Midwestern volunteer in March 1862. "I could not help send a runaway nigger back. I am blamed if I could." The blame that many Union soldiers felt at being implicated in slavery was complicated and compounded by the outrage they experienced when they discovered that these very same men and women who had been returned to bondage were being mobilized against them by their Confederate enemy. It seemed folly for the Union soldiers to deny themselves the resources that their enemy was using freely, and, indeed, assisting their enemy in maintaining those resources.

The lessons learned by common soldiers in the early years of the war were soon passed on to the officers. The protection and employment offered to fugitive slaves by individual northern soldiers created numerous conflicts between slaveholders and the Union army, embroiling officers in a disagreeable contest whose resolution required considerable time and effort. Slaveholders, many of them flaunting their Unionist credentials, demanded that northern troops return fugitives who were taken into their encampments. When regimental officers would not or could not comply, slave owners blustered about their connections that reached to the highest levels in Washington. Generally, the bluster was just that, but, often enough, officers in the Union army felt the weight of high authority upon them. Officers in the middle ranks not only bore the brunt of the soldier's frustration with federal policy but also the sting of official abuse from on high. Many apologists for federal policies soon came to believe they contradicted their experience and good sense. Field officers found themselves in the uncomfortable position of having to enforce what they disdained. They objected particularly to being compelled to doing the slave master's dirty work, and they particularly disliked being demeaned before their own men. The high-handed demand of slaveholders turned many federal officers into the slave's champions.

When federal policy toward fugitive slaves finally changed during the summer of 1862, one could almost hear an audible sigh of relief from the Union officers' corps. "This whole thing of guarding rebels' property is played out," wrote one officer. "We have guarded their homes and property long enough. The only way to put down this rebellion is to hurt the instigators and abettors of it. Slavery must be cleaned out." Faced with the conflicting demands between their own needs for labor and the requirements of federal policy, the desire to protect hapless fugitives and the demand of unionist slave owners, many Union soldiers and officers searched for a way to stand clear of the entire business or, in the idiom of the day, to be neither slave catcher nor slave stealer.

Union policy toward slaves beginning in the fall of 1861 and running through the spring of 1862 was designed to eliminate what one officer called the "devilish nigger question" by excluding fugitives from Union lines. But slaves refused to surrender their belief that the federal army would be a refuge from slavery. They would not let federal soldiers evade the central reality of the war. Slaves continued to press themselves on soldiers, bringing gifts of food, information, and, of course, labor. There always seemed to be a few Yankee soldiers—for whatever reason—who would shelter runaway slaves and a handful who encouraged slave flight. Even when the fugitives were denied entry into federal lines, they camped outside, perhaps just far enough to avoid expulsion by federal commanders but just close enough to avoid capture by Confederate soldiers and sympathizers. Meanwhile, they were alert to ways to turn the military conflict to their own advantage, and slaves continued to search the seams of federal policy looking for an opening—the ascent of a sympathetic commander or a crisis that might inflate the value of their knowledge or their muscle. They learned the letter of the law so that some could recite passages from memory the House Resolution of July 1861, the additional Article of War of March 1862, the First Confiscation Act of August 1861, or the Second Confiscation Act of July 1862, all of which made it much easier for slaves to remain with Union troops.

Time and time again, slaves forced federal officers and their soldiers to make choices; choices that became easier as the Union army need for labor grew. Change came—not all at once—but it came. The lessons that slaves taught individual soldiers on the ground, in their encampments, and in the border States ascended the ranks of the federal chain of command, and, by November 1861, they had reached Lincoln's cabinet for the first time. Secretary of War Simon Cameron publicly endorsed the policy to arm slaves to fight for the Union army. Lincoln quieted Cameron and packed him off to Russia as United States ambassador. But the slaves continued undeterred nonetheless.

This slow shift of federal policy gained momentum as the Union army penetrated more deeply into the Confederacy, where the slaveholders were not reluctant Unionists but outright rebels. In these circumstances, many field commanders became quick learners. Their respect for the old order yielded to a willingness to challenge the rights of slave masters and, finally, to a firm determination to destroy slavery. Others, of course, learned more slowly, more imperfectly, and, some learned not at all. The latter found few promotions or active commands. By the summer of 1862, Abraham Lincoln made it clear that he too would not be left behind.

Integrating this story of the slave's struggle and the slave's action—their failures and their successes—into the story of our sacred ground is not a task that should be seen as something simply to attract additional visitors, be they black or white, to our battlefields. The task before us is not to politicize our history. The task is not to make our history more politically correct. It is not even to assure funding of the battlefields in an often politically poisonous environment. The task is to interpret history in a way that is more inclusive, to make a better history, and a richer history. It is to make a history in which all Americans can see themselves, so that the past may, at long last, be past.

Questions and Answers

Question: We know that the Emancipation Proclamation only legally had an effect on slaves in the areas that were under rebellion. But the actual effect of the Proclamation must have been greater, since many people thought it had freed slaves. I was wondering if you had any comment on the actual impact of the Emancipation, as opposed to its legal effects.

Answer: The Emancipation Proclamation had an extraordinary impact far beyond its legal bounds. It was said by the great historian, Richard Hofstadter, that the Emancipation Proclamation had the moral impact of a bill of lading. Lincoln, despite his enormous abilities with language, made the Emancipation Proclamation an extraordinarily flat, passionless document. I think Lincoln did that because he understood that the Emancipation Proclamation did not need any rhetorical help. It was powerful enough standing on its own.

The most significant part of the Emancipation Proclamation was Lincoln's willingness to accept black men in the Union Army. That distinguished the Emancipation Proclamation from his earlier preliminary Emancipation Proclamation. It distinguished it from the Second Confiscation Act, which otherwise had much the same effect as the Emancipation Proclamation. It was the willingness to take black men in the Union Army, which began almost immediately in January 1863 with the recruitment of the Massachusetts 54th Regiment, as well as black regiments in Connecticut and Rhode Island, which transformed the federal army. The black men who entered the Union Army, more than anyone else, were the people who transformed the war for the Union into a war for freedom. They made it clear that they and their families certainly were not going to be slaves. Eventually Congress acquiesced to their understanding.

Question: Do you believe the subject of slavery should be integrated into all Civil War interpretations, or is it better to offer a separate or more expansive program specifically about slavery?

Answer: I think what the practice of history is about, is asking questions, then trying to answer questions, and then trying to connect the answers. The more connections the better your history. That is, the more seamless, the larger the amount of information you can encompass in the understanding of any phenomena, the better that history. This is true universally. It certainly is true about the question of slavery in the American Civil War. This combination is not a mixture. It is a compound in the scientific sense. In other words, the issue we have been discussing cannot be separated. We do not even have a choice whether to integrate the history of slavery into the history of the Civil War. The history of slavery is part of the Civil War and the history of the Civil War is part of the history of slavery. So, these things are in fact of one piece.

Question: You said that slavery was not a shame. Wasn't slavery degrading in itself, and wasn't there degradation and shame in slavery by its very nature?

Answer: Yes, however, I was trying to distinguish between slavery's purposes and slavery's effect. Slavery had many effects. It certainly was degrading. Both slave and master, as such, understood that. But in its origins and original purpose, the function of slavery was not to degrade. Slaves were not dragged across the Atlantic Ocean for the purpose of ridicule, shame, degradation, or dehumanization. They were dragged across the Atlantic Ocean to work. This fact is critical to understanding slavery and its function in American society. Once slavery was established, it touched everyone and eventually became the center not simply of a system of labor but of a way of life. This is why slavery was so difficult to eliminate and why it eventually took a civil war to destroy. It is also why slavery has cast such a long shadow over our own society, and why, in fact, we are here today to discuss the integration of slavery into our history on our sacred ground.

Question: Would you please comment on the black soldiers who fought for the Confederacy? It seems a bit of a controversy in that they were fighting for a country that was keeping them in bondage.

Answer: Well, the safest thing to say about this controversy is that it is a non-controversy. I do not believe there were many such black men in Confederate ranks. We know there were over 200,000 black men who served in the Union army and navy—over 135,000 of them were slaves. There were at most a handful of slaves who served in the Confederate army. These men identified with the Confederacy for a variety of reasons, mostly because they had long identified with white society. In the last month of the war, there was an attempt to recruit slaves into the Confederate army en masse. There was, in fact, legislation passed to that effect. There is very little evidence that any slaves were recruited. It is very difficult to imagine that anybody, whatever their color or whatever their status, joining the Confederate Army in March 1865.

Question: Do you believe that the already poorly funded interpretation programs at the National Parks will be severely curtailed by taking resources away from the literal mission, and, in part, supplanting that with the general social histories? If that is the case, why interpret the battlefield?

Answer: From my experience, there never is enough money to do the job. I presume it is true with National Parks as well. But I also understand that this is not a zero sum game—that by attending one matter you cannot attend another. Rather by doing both things (address the history of the battle site and the history of slavery) you will be able to do both of them better. You can do them more efficiently in an intellectual sense in that you will be able to tell a larger history. It does not appear to me that it is possible to tell the history of the battlefields without telling the history of slavery.

Question: You talked about the future, and we also know that historians deal with the future. I would like to know what you think this speech would sound like if given twenty-five years from now. What changes might you expect in our understanding of slavery?

Answer: I have no better ability to predict the future than anybody in this audience. What I would say is that I think what we see in this moment, which in some ways is represented by the task assigned the National Park Service, an opportunity to change our history and to change American posterity. Right now we don't have any models for talking about slavery. I expect in twenty-five years we will.

Question: Slavery as a legalized institution collapsed in late nineteenth-century Brazil without a war. Is the Brazilian discourse on race different than the United States discourse? If so, how?

Answer: The Brazilian discourse is very different than ours. Brazilians define race differently than we do. We are believers in the one-drop rule. Brazil has a very different definition of who is black and who is white. In doing this, they draw upon their experience, one example of which is that there was no civil war in Brazil to end slavery in 1888. But there was an enormous amount of violence. Indeed, my own studies of emancipation in comparative perspective have yet to locate a place in which slavery ended without violence. Slavery is an institution of violence, and the sad truth is that an institution of violence cannot end without violence itself. And this was true in Brazil and the Brazilians, like ourselves, paid and are paying the price.

Suggestions for further reading:

Berlin, Ira. *Many Thousands Gone: The First Two Centuries of Slavery in North America*. Cambridge: Harvard University Press, 1998.

_____, et al., eds. *Remembering Slavery: African Americans Talk About Their Personal Experiences of Slavery and Emancipation*. New York: W. W. Norton, 1998.

Blassingame, John. *The Slave Community: Plantation Life in the Antebellum South*. New York: Oxford University Press, 1979.

Frey, Sylvia. *Water from the Rock: Black Resistance in a Revolutionary Age*. Princeton: Princeton University Press, 1991.

Genovese, Eugene D. *Roll, Jordan, Roll: The World the Slaves Made*. New York: Random House, 1976.

Gutman, Herbert G. *The Black Family in Slavery and Freedom. 1750-1925*. New York: Random House, 1977.

Kolchin, Peter. *American Slavery, 1619-1877*. New York: Hill and Wang, 1994.

Levine, Lawrence. *Black Culture and Black Consciousness: Afro-American Folk Thought from Slavery to Freedom*. New York: Oxford University Press, 1978.

Morgan, Philip D. *Slave Counterpoint: Black Culture in the Eighteenth Century Chesapeake and Lowcountry*. Chapel Hill: University of North Carolina Press, 1998.

Rose, Willie Lee, ed. *A Documentary History of Slavery in North America*. Athens: University of Georgia Press, 1999.

Stampp, Kenneth M. *The Peculiar Institution: Slavery in the Ante-Bellum South*. New York: Vintage Books, 1989.

HEALING, HERITAGE AND HISTORY

The National Park Service has a double burden in interpreting the history of the Civil War. We interpret the history of the war itself and its context, but we also preserve and interpret the history of many of the places where the war was fought. Many of these sites are filled with memorials and markers with evidence of the extraordinary continuing importance of the war in American life. Americans are continuously engaged with the war, with the memory of the war, and with the issues and legacies that the war has generated for us. Professors Blight and Linenthal offer their perspectives on the legacy of the Civil War as represented in monuments and battlefields.

Introduced by Richard Rabinowitz, President,
American History Workshop

I. HEALING AND HISTORY: BATTLEFIELDS AND THE PROBLEM OF CIVIL WAR MEMORY

by David W. Blight

In this historic room today, the place where the Civil War's culminating tragedy took place, we probably all share a set of passions. We all love or appreciate the past. Sometimes we just have that passion for the pastness of the past; we love things that are old and speak to us from another age. Sometimes it is a passion for detail, for the wonderful stuff of research, the joy of discovery, the relationships of real people, real events, and real documents. Sometimes it is a passion for the truth. Perhaps we share a passion for language as well, for the story for the beauty and music of words. The other passion that we may share is the one we are about here today. It is probably our least holy and least sexy passion—our quest to understand context. It is hard to make context sound exciting, but without it we take the risk of having no history at all. Without context, we can end up with only objects to examine; we risk simple, single, causal explanations of the past. Or, if we do not pursue context, we may allow our students and our audiences to abandon explanation or interpretation altogether in favor of what we believe or wish to be accurate about the past. Of course, a tendency may exist in all of us to make the past what it needs to be in order to serve our present. But we have come here to challenge ourselves to broaden the contextual interpretations of the Civil War at the sacred sites where the conflict was fought.

My assignment is to speak about battlefields as sites of "healing" in American history. By looking at the history of how some of our battlefields became such important sites of commemoration we may better understand how they have been used as places of reconciliation and healing, sometimes at the expense of other kinds of learning. Frederick Douglass left us many challenges that might serve as clarion calls for our collective enterprise. On Memorial Day, 1878, Douglass gave a speech in Madison Square in New York City. It was one year after the political compromise of 1877 that had settled the sectional dispute over the presidential election of 1876. The "end" of Reconstruction, politically, had taken place and the nation seemed to be reconciling all over American culture. Douglass was deeply worried about the future of black civil rights, the freed people's liberties—the very meaning for which, in his view, the Civil War had been fought. He was worried that too many Americans were losing an understanding of the deepest context of the war and its consequences. The conflict of 1861-65, said Douglass, had been "a war of ideas, a battle of principles...a war between the old and the new, slavery and freedom, barbarism and civilization." It "was not a fight," he insisted, "between rapacious birds and ferocious beasts, a mere display of brute courage and endurance, but it was a war between men of thought, as well as of action, and in dead earnest for something beyond the battlefield."

In 1961, the Southern poet and novelist, Robert Penn Warren, in his *The Legacy of the Civil War*, offered a similar challenge. "The Civil War is our felt history—history lived in the national imagination," said Warren. "Somewhere in their bones," he declared, most Americans have a storehouse of "lessons" drawn from the Civil War. Exactly what those lessons should be, and who should determine them, has been the most contested question in American historical memory at least since 1863. Among those lessons, wrote Warren, is the realization that "slavery looms up mountainously" in the story, "and cannot be talked away." But Warren acknowledged another lesson of equal importance for Americans of all persuasions: "When one is happy in forgetfulness, facts get forgotten." Or, as William Dean Howells once put it: "What the American public always wants is a tragedy with a happy ending."

Americans faced an overwhelming task after the Civil War and emancipation: how to understand the tangled relationship between two profound ideas—healing and justice. On some level, both had to occur; but given the potency of white supremacy in nineteenth-century America, these two aims never developed in historical balance. One might conclude that this imbalance between the outcomes of sectional healing and racial justice were simply America's inevitable historical condition, and celebrate the remarkable swiftness of the reunion. But theories of inevitability—of irrepressible conflicts or irrepressible reconciliations—are rarely satisfying. Human reconciliations—when tragically divided people can unify again around aspirations, ideas, and the positive bonds of nationalism—are to be cherished. But sometimes reconciliations come with terrible costs, both intentional and unseen. The sectional reunion after so horrible a civil war was a political triumph by the late nineteenth century; but it could not have been achieved without the re-subjugation of many of those people the war had freed from centuries of bondage. This is the tragedy lingering on the margins and infesting the heart of American history from Appomattox to World War I.

For many whites, especially veterans and their family members, healing from the war was simply not the same proposition as doing justice to the four million emancipated slaves and their descendants. On the other hand, a simple justice, a fair chance to exercise their basic rights, and secure access to land and livelihood were all most blacks ever demanded of Reconstruction and beyond. The rub, of course, was that there were so many warring definitions of healing in the South, and the nation's collective memory had never been so shattered.

In the wake of the Civil War, there were no "Truth and Reconciliation" commissions through which to process memories of either slavery for blacks or the experience of total war for southern whites. Defeated white southerners and black former slaves faced each other on the ground, seeing and knowing the awful chasm between their experiences, unaware that any path would lead to their reconciliation. Yankee and Confederate soldiers would eventually find a smoother path to bonds of fraternalism and mutual glory. As is always the case in any society trying to master the most conflict-ed elements of its past, healing and justice had to happen in history and through politics. Americans have had to work through the meaning of their Civil War in the only place it could happen—in the politics of memory. As long as we have a politics of race in America, we will have a politics of Civil War memory, and likely a politics of how we forge that memory at our battlefields.

For Americans broadly, the Civil War has been a defining event upon which we have often imposed unity and continuity. As a culture we have often preferred its music and pathos to its endur-ing challenges, the theme of reconciled conflict to resurgent, unresolved legacies. The greatest enthus-iasts for Civil War history and memory often displace complicated consequences by endlessly focusing on the contest itself. Over time, Americans have needed deflections from the deeper mean-ings of the Civil War. It haunts us still; we feel it, to borrow from Warren, but often do not face it.

In the half century after the war, as the sections reconciled, by and large, the races divided. Race was so deeply at the root of the war's causes and consequences, and so powerful a source of division in American social psychology, that it served as the antithesis of a culture of reconciliation. The mem-ory of slavery, emancipation, and the Fourteenth and Fifteenth amendments never fit well into a developing narrative in which the Old and New South were romanticized and welcomed back to a new nationalism, and in which devotion alone made everyone right, and no one truly wrong in the remembered Civil War. Persistent discussion of the "Race Problem" across the political and ideo-logical spectrum throughout the late nineteenth century meant that American society could not eas-ily remember its "Civil War problem," or a "Blue-Gray problem." Battlefields served particularly well as the places where this separation in memory became most explicit; no "race problem" was allowed to invade the increasingly mystical reconciliation of the "Blue" and the "Gray" on the landscapes that the aging veterans had rendered sacred.

In a popular novel, *Cease Firing* (1912), the Southern writer Mary Johnston, a Virginian imbued with "lost cause" tradition and a determination to represent its complexity, imagined a dialogue that may have captured the memory most Americans—then and even now—want to embrace about the Civil War. On the last page of the book, Robert E. Lee's Army of Northern Virginia is retreating west toward its final collapse and surrender at Appomattox Court House in the last week of the war. The April breezes are not yet warm and the rivers to be forded still run cold. One Confederate soldier asks another what he thinks it all means. "I think that we were both right and both wrong," says the vet-eran of many battles, "and that, in the beginning, each side might have been more patient and much wiser. Life and history, and right and wrong and minds of men look out of more windows than we used to think! Did you never hear of the shield that had two sides and both were precious metal?"

There was, of course, no lack of honor on either side in that fateful surrender at Appomattox in 1865. And Johnston captured an honest soldiers' sentiment that had reverberated down through vet-erans' memory for decades. But outside of this pathos and the endearing mutuality of sacrifice among soldiers that came to dominate national memory, another process was at work—the denigration of black humanity and dignity, and the attempted erasure of emancipation from the national narrative of what the war had been about. That other process led the black scholar and editor, W. E. B. Du Bois, to conclude in the same year as Johnston's novel that "this country has had its appetite for facts on the Negro problem spoiled by sweets." Deflections and evasions, careful remembering and nec-essary forgetting, and embittered and irreconcilable versions of experience, are all the stuff of histor-ical memory.

Have Civil War battlefields been sites of healing and reconciliation? Well, over time, in a variety of ways, they have become just that in our national culture. But at first, they were places of death and destruction, graveyards and sites of haunted memory, for both the victors and the vanquished. In the immediate wake of the war the battlefields, in combination with devastated Southern cities, made America for the first time, a land with ruins. Unlike the haunting, destroyed abbeys of the English Civil War of the seventeenth century or Rome's ancient, majestic city of ruins, America's destruction was brand new—new, but instantaneously historic, and, therefore, at many battlefields and burial grounds, sacred. Americans were now a people with so much bloody history that the United States would forever be a modern society, burdened by a historic landscape—full of sites it would have to memorialize, romanticize, and even explain.

No one understood this better than defeated white Southerners; but their ruins inspired different reactions, depending on time and perspective. In October 1865, just after his release from a five-month imprisonment in Boston, former Confederate Vice-President, Alexander H. Stephens, rode a slow train southward. In northern Virginia, he found that "the desolation of the country from Alexandria to near Charlottesville was horrible to behold." When Stephens reached northern Georgia, his native state, he was again shocked: "War has left a terrible impression on the whole country to Atlanta. The desolation is heart-sickening. Fences gone, fields all a-waste, houses burnt." As time passed during Reconstruction, other southerners, such as Father Abram Ryan, known as the "Poet Priest of the Lost Cause," found inspiration and spiritual renewal in the South's ruins. "A land without ruins is a land without memories," said Ryan. Through its battlefield landscapes, he imagined, the South would achieve its "consecrated cornet of sorrow," and with time win "the sympathy of the heart and of history." From such landscapes and from such sentiments, the defeated Confederacy did attain a kind of exotic and romantic niche in American

✳

COLD HARBOR, VIRGINIA:
AFRICAN AMERICANS COLLECTING BONES OF SOLDIERS KILLED IN BATTLE.

popular imagination, an idea Tony Horwitz uncovered and may have immortalized in his *Confederates in the Attic.*

In the wake of the war, thousands of northern readers learned of the condition of the defeated South, its material and political condition, as well as its famous battlefields, from northern travel writers. In *The South: A Tour of Its Battlefields and Ruined Cities* (1866), the novelist and poet John T. Trowbridge wrote the longest and most lyrical of such accounts. Trowbridge was one of the first battlefield tourists; he began his journeys in late August, 1865, at Gettysburg. Guided by the local civilian hero of the battle, John Burns, Trowbridge began his tour on Cemetery Hill. The supreme "stillness" of the summer day was broken only by the "perpetual click-click" sound of stonecutters preparing headstones in the soldiers' cemetery. The scene moved Trowbridge deeply; it was already "the time-hallowed place of the dead." He felt an "overpowering sense of the horror and wickedness of war" as he watched workmen still digging trenches and laying foundations for gravestones. He watched a veritable production line making stones lettered "Unknown," and felt compelled to contemplate the meaning of it all. Trowbridge could have been speaking for thousands of tourists in our own time who visit this most famous of American battlefields. "Grown accustomed to the waste of life through years of war," he wrote, "we learn to think too lightly of such sacrifices. 'So many killed,'—with that brief sentence we glide over the unimaginably fearful, and pass on to other details." Trowbridge demanded meaning from what he observed, not merely a feeling of the grandeur of the massive fight. But the meaning remained to him "vague and uncertain. It lies before us like one of those unidentified heroes," he said, "hidden from sight, deep-buried, mysterious, its headstones lettered Unknown."

Cemetery Hill at Gettysburg moved Trowbridge to ponder warily the nation's rebirth in that first summer after the war. "Will it ever rise?" he asked. The "uncounted thousands" of dead soldiers, he wrote, had "confronted, for their country's sake, that awful uncertainty." Strolling reflectively among the cemetery workmen, Trowbridge "looked into one of the trenches... and saw the ends of the coffins protruding. It was silent and dark down there." It was as though the elusive meaning of the war was in that trench; the coffin captured the observer as no abstract monument ever could. "I chose out one coffin from among the rest," remembered Trowbridge, "and thought of him whose dust it contained, your brother and mine, although we never knew him." The author tried to think of the man's childhood, his parents and homelife. But he could only conclude: "I could not know; in this world, none will ever know." Trowbridge altered his gaze, resumed his tour, and moved on to "other details" further South.

In Richmond and other places in Virginia, Trowbridge interviewed a number of former slaveholders and former slaves, and he began to "know" more and think more clearly about the meaning of the war. But so often at Civil War battlefields, Americans are still walking in Trowbridge's footsteps, observing and moved, but not knowing why so many men died on those beautiful landscapes. We cannot see the coffins protruding from the ground anymore, nor hear the stone-cutter's hammer; we need help in bridging the gap between the graves and their meanings. The most important forms of healing are probably those that come from a combination of emotion and knowledge that instructs and even surprises us, rather from that which confirms what we already want to believe.

Another remarkable series of travel accounts was the result of a three-month tour in 1869 by Russell Conwell, a 26-year-old Union veteran, writing for the *Boston Daily Evening Traveler*. Many of Conwell's twenty-five extensive letters were reflections on the battlefield sites or cemeteries he visited. Stunned at how "shattered and ruined" much of Virginia's countryside still appeared, he remarked that the war had "transformed the 'Garden of the South' into the 'Graveyard of America.'" He talked to farmers whose plows kept disturbing the remains of dead soldiers. Conwell entertained his readers with a combination of the sacred and the humorous. Who could resist his story of attending the wedding of a crippled Union veteran from New Hampshire and a young Virginia girl who, during the Peninsula Campaign, along with an old black woman, had nursed the badly wounded soldier to health? The rural wedding scene included a black fiddler providing music for this particular reconciliation among common folk. Conwell observed half-buried ruins and earthworks everywhere. Around old battlefields he encountered a steady stream of lead and bone hunters who sold their scrap findings to eke out a living. At Cold Harbor battlefield, he met "several Negroes with large sacks, collecting the bones of dead horses which they sold to the bone-grinders of Richmond."

When Conwell reached Charleston, South Carolina, he visited the remains of Fort Wagner on Morris Island. There he met an older black man who claimed to have been a member of the 54th Massachusetts and wounded in its famous charge of July 1863. The black veteran and his family lived in a "bomb-proof" nearby and made a living "digging for old iron in the sand." "The products of his industry," remarked Conwell, "reminded us of the stacks in a New England hay field. He sells it by the ton...." In this image of the Reconstruction South in 1869, we are reminded that old battlefields can have deep and unexpected contexts. Before leaving the beach by the remains of Fort Wagner, Conwell described "old haversacks, belts, bayonet scabbards, and shoes" still strewn on the sand. At his feet, human skulls and bones rolled up in the surf. The skulls "lay grinning," he said, "and filled us with sad sensations, which still haunt our dreams. The sad and the beautiful, how strangely combined!" Conwell's Yankee partisanship flowed through as he departed. The whole scene, he believed, was a living memorial to "the cause of human freedom."

A visitor to today's battlefields will meet no veterans as bone-collectors, no skulls will wash up in the surf at his or her feet. We will not encounter actual haversacks from battle strewn on the ground. In the interpretation of battle sites, we may not be confronted with images or information about a black veteran scraping out a life in an old bomb-proof, collecting mounds of metal—we may never know what followed from those battles in the aftermath of the war, among whites and blacks, on the ground in the South. "The sad and the beautiful, strangely combined," Conwell put it aptly—it was always one of my own first reactions when I visited battlefields as a kid and as a young adult. But from the metaphors Trowbridge and Conwell provide—gazing at skulls, talking to black bone-collectors, and pondering the meanings of coffins at the Gettysburg cemetery—we ought to be able to imagine new ways to enrich the story, to broaden the historical meanings we take from these sacred sites.

During the first decade or so after the war, Civil War veterans on both sides tried to forge new lives. Veterans' organizations and reunions lagged until the late 1870s. Women, South and North, tended to lead memorial activity. But especially in the 1880s, battlefields increasingly became sites of regimental reunions, a growing industry of monument building, the object of detailed mapping (such as John Bachelder's life-long work at Gettysburg), and eventually a growing array of Blue-Gray reunions. Bitterness between Yankee and Confederate veterans could still emerge, especially over such issues as the possible return of battle flags, and the long-standing reticence of most ex-Confederates to return to Gettysburg at all.

But aging soldiers shared much in the Gilded Age; a kind of "culture of character" emerged as a core ideology that knit them together. Old soldiers tended to measure each other as preservers of an older, more wholesome society, uncorrupted by materialism, and rooted in individual honor. They came to see their war experience as a special shared possession, and the battlefields where they reassembled twenty or thirty years after the fact, as their own sites of healing. Upon his return to Gettysburg in 1884, Samuel Armstrong, a Union veteran and founder of the black college, Hampton Institute, recollected the agony of his battle experience. "Those days were full of horrible sights," he said. "Yet in all these sickening scenes there was, I think, no hatred; the malice and rascality engendered by war is at the rear. There is a certain mutual respect among those who accept the wager of battle." Armstrong may have underestimated the "hatreds" men felt at the moment of truth in battle. He had not yet read Edward Porter Alexander's memoir in which the former Confederate general wrote honestly about his joy in killing Yankees and seeing them dead on the ground. But in the mutuality of sacrifice, in the shared claim to a special realm of experience and manliness, in their obsessions for detail in preserving and mapping battlefields, veterans themselves became America's first Civil War "buffs." They began to transform those battlefields into places of sectional healing, though rarely if ever places of racial healing.

In 1888, George Kilmer, a member of the Abraham Lincoln post of the Grand Army of the Republic in New York published in *Century Magazine* a list of some twenty-four Blue-Gray reunions of one kind or another between 1881 and 1887. He then updated the list with three or four more he discovered from the 1870s. Kilmer believed these gatherings reflected a shared "faith" among soldiers that increased "business relations" and intersectional migration had helped foment these events. Some meetings consisted of southern and northern veterans' groups touring the other section's cities and being ceremonially received by their former foes. Some occurred in the aftermath of the assassination of President James Garfield in 1881. Some occurred at historical anniversaries such as the Bunker Hill centennial in Boston in 1875. But increasingly these reunions met at battlefields, often on anniversaries, such as at Fredericksburg, Chancellorsville, and the Wilderness in Virginia and at Kennesaw Mountain in Georgia in October 1887.

At Gettysburg the early history of Blue-Gray fraternalism was mixed. A first attempt in 1874 was abandoned when it became clear that it was simply too early for soldiers to mingle at the scene of such sensitive memories. Reconstruction politics also delayed such fraternalism; as long as the "bloody shirt" was so useful on both sides in the struggles over the meaning of the war, Blue-Gray reunions were not easy to organize. Confederates were also deeply divided among themselves between Virginians and North Carolinians over the responsibility for defeat at Gettysburg. But by 1887, on the twenty-fourth anniversary of the battle, some 500 members of the Philadelphia Brigade veterans' organization met with some 200 survivors of Pickett's Division. They met in an elaborate ceremony in the town square to shake hands. Then after speeches acknowledging mutual valor, they gathered out at the "High Water Mark" where they had met in 1863 in some of the most celebrated combat of the war. They pitched tents and spent the night, exchanging stories, hats and mementos, including for a few, locks of hair. One reporter remarked that it was hard to tell who was from North or South.

All was not sweetness in Blue-Gray relations, however, especially when the Democratic President, Grover Cleveland, not a veteran, suggested the return of battle flags. An 1888 attempt at a larger reunion on the twenty-fifth anniversary was a disappointment. Some Union veterans were not yet ready to share the Gettysburg landscape with Confederates. "No God-knows-who-was-right bosh must be tolerated at Gettysburg," wrote the editor of a veterans' journal. "The men who won the victory there were eternally right, and the men who were defeated were eternally wrong." With time, though, an "everyone was right" bosh did overtake the practice of Blue-Gray fraternalism.

Sometimes reunions were explicitly organized for intersectional political and business dealings. On Memorial Day weekend in 1895, a huge Blue-Gray affair met in Chicago to unveil a large monument in Oakwood Cemetery to the 6,229 Confederate soldiers who had died during the war at the Camp Douglas prison compound. The event was the brainchild of John C. Underwood, a Kentucky Confederate veteran and business entrepreneur. Underwood's earlier efforts at such gatherings in Philadelphia in 1885 and Columbus, Ohio in 1889 had largely failed. But in 1890 he moved his "headquarters" to Chicago, and helped found the "Ex-Confederate Association of Chicago." Many surviving ex-Confederate generals were honored in receptions at the Palmer House hotel, including James Longstreet, Fitzhugh Lee, Wade Hampton (the latter two former governors of their states by then), and Stephen D. Lee of Mississippi. A crowd estimated at 100,000 participated in the parade and unveiling ceremonies, and Wade Hampton was the keynote speaker. Chicago papers gushed with admiration for the event. Even the progressive *Inter-Ocean* marvelled that "yesterday it mattered not who wore the blue or wore the gray."

Such spectacles were emotionally irresistible to most people. But other motives animated participants as well. The leader of the Chicago Citizens' Committee welcomed the Confederate soldiers in the interest of "closer commercial relations and business union... a larger degree of investment of capital [by the North] in the vast resources of the southern states." Responding for the Confederate veterans, Stephen Lee said: "We invite you again to invade us, not with your bayonets this time, but with your business. We want to hear in our land the voices of your industry...." But other themes had to be put to rest first. When Underwood himself spoke at the banquet, he declared the purpose of the reunion to be "harmonious forgetfulness." "It is not now profitable," he announced, "to discuss the right or wrong of the past... neither should the question be raised as to the morals of Massachusetts selling her slaves and South Carolina holding hers, nor as to the profit of merchandising the negro on the block in New York or for the sugar cane fields of the Mississippi coasts...." In this vision of Blue-Gray fraternalism, slavery was everyone's and no one's responsibility. America's bloody racial history was to be banished from consciousness; the only notions of equality were soldiers' heroism and the exchange of the business deal.

Later that same year (1895), one of the most spectacular reunions of the decade occurred at the dedication of the Chickamauga and Chattanooga National Military Park, September 18-20. An estimated 50,000 people attended, including the vice-president of the United States, Adlai Stevenson, numerous states governors and many surviving generals from both sides. Among the many speakers was General Lew Wallace, author of *Ben Hur* and the former governor of the Territory of New Mexico. Capturing the tone of the reunion, Wallace asked "Remembrance! Remembrance of what? Not the cause, but the heroism it invoked." And, Alabama Governor, W. C. Oates, a Confederate veteran, told his southern comrades to stand "proud," for "they fought for a just cause, which though lost, was partially won." Oates actually addressed slavery, though he acknowledged it was the "pandora's box of American politics." He painted a picture of benevolent masters fated to their lot. Cruelty existed in slavery, Oates admitted, but "the negroes simply passed through the fiery furnace of slavery to reach civilization, which was the only road by which they could have obtained it." Some veterans were thus willing to speak of the war's causes, contexts and meanings at battlefields, but often only in ways that fit neatly into the imperatives of an emerging white supremacist society.

One of the contexts for the Chickamauga reunion was that on the very same day in Atlanta, Booker T. Washington was delivering his "Atlanta Compromise" speech, urging black and white southerners to "cast down their buckets where they are." Washington electrified the nation's press and thousands of readers with perhaps the most important sectional reconciliation speech ever delivered, rooted, of course, in the futile dream that racial reconciliation could be forged in mutual economic progress.

Let me offer one further example of the uses of battlefields for national reconciliation. As it stood in the general American culture in the early twentieth century, Civil War memory never saw a more fully orchestrated expression than that at Gettysburg on the battle's fiftieth anniversary in July 1913. With their railway tickets paid for by the government, more than 53,000 veterans came to Gettysburg—both Blue and Gray. Veterans came from every state except two. The states and the federal government appropriated well over $2,000,000 to put on this remarkable festival of harmony and reconciliation. The reunion came off as a kind of public avowal of a glorious fight that led to greater national unity.

All the state governors, as well as many surviving officers, spoke during the four days of the reunion. Governor William Hodges Mann, himself a Confederate veteran, struck the keynote of the reunion. "We are not here to discuss the genesis of the war," he declared, "but men who have tried each other in the storm and smoke of battle are here to discuss the great fight. We came here, I say, not to discuss what caused the war of 1861-65, but to talk over the events of the battle as man to man." No time or space was allowed at the four-day spectacle for discussion of causes and consequences. There was no rhetoric about emancipation or the unresolved history of Reconstruction. Nor was there any consideration of the war's second great outcome by 1913—the nation's disastrous abandonment of racial reconciliation. The "Peace Jubilee," as the reunion was called, was a Jim Crow reunion. There is no evidence that any black veterans attended or were welcome in spite of what you see in episode eleven of Ken Burns's film series on the Civil War. So far as can be determined, there were no black veterans at the 1913 gathering of the Blue and the Gray. The only blacks in attendance were laborers who helped build the tent city, who constructed and cleaned the latrines, and who dispensed blankets to the white veterans. This stunning and photogenic gathering of old veterans, which was covered by the national and international press for several days, featured an enfeebled re-enactment by actual participants of part of Pickett's Charge and the familiar handshakes across the stone walls on Cemetery Ridge. There had never been such a spectacle of resolution and patriotism on this scale in America. "Thank God for Gettysburg, Hosanna!" proclaimed the *Louisville Courier Journal*. "God bless us everyone, alike the Blue and the Gray.... The world ne'er witnessed such a site as this. Beholding, can we say happy is the nation that hath no history."

At a time when lynching had developed into a social ritual of its own horrifying kind (the National Association for the Advancement of Colored People counted 70 in 1913), and when the American apartheid had become fully entrenched, many black leaders and editors found the sectional love feast at Gettysburg more than they could bear. "A Reunion of whom?" asked the *Washington Bee*. Only those who "fought for the preservation of the Union and the extinction of slavery," or also those who "fought to destroy the Union and perpetuate slavery, and who are now employing every artifice... known to deceit... to propagate a national sentiment in favor of their nefarious contention that emancipation, reconstruction and enfranchisement are a dismal failure." Black responses to such reunions as that at Gettysburg in 1913 and a host of other similar events demonstrated how fundamentally at odds black memories were by then from the spirit and character of the national reunion. In that contradiction lay an American tragedy not yet fully told by 1913 and considered out of place at Blue-Gray reunions.

African American responses to the 1913 Gettysburg reunion were especially telling in the context of the Wilson administration's efforts that very summer to aggressively re-segregate federal agencies in Washington, D.C. Woodrow Wilson, just elected president in 1912, and inaugurated that spring of 1913, came to the Pennsylvania town on July 4, the last day of the reunion, to give his own Gettysburg address. Wilson did not really want to come; he wanted no part of this festival of sectional peace, and as the first southerner elected president since the Civil War, he wished not to have to test the politics of such an event. Up until about four days before the reunion he still planned not to attend. But one of his aides said to him in effect: "You don't get it; you don't quite understand what is going on up at Gettysburg. You need to be there."

President Wilson rode into Gettysburg by train, was quickly put into an open car, and whisked out to the battlefield where a huge tent awaited him, filled with some 12,000 of the veterans. He walked into the tent accompanied on either side by a Union veteran and a Confederate veteran, each holding their respective flags. In his brief speech, Wilson declared it "an impertinence to discourse upon how the battle went, how it ended," or even "what it signified." Wilson's charge, he claimed, was to comprehend what the fifty years since the battle had meant. His answer struck the mystic chord that most Americans were prepared to hear:

> *They have meant peace and union and vigor, and the maturity and might of a great nation. How wholesome and healing the peace had been! We have found one another again as brothers and comrades, in arms, enemies no longer, generous friends rather, our battles long past, the* **quarrel forgotten** *– except that we shall not forget the splendid valor, the manly devotion of the men then arrayed against one another, now grasping hands and smiling into each other's eyes. How complete the Union has become and how dear to all of us, how unquestioned, how benign and majestic, as state after state has been added to this, our great family of free men.*

Wilson's great gift for ambiguity was in perfect form. The Civil War had thus become the "quarrel forgotten" on the statute books of Jim Crow America. A nation can have too much memory, but a nation can also forget too much.

Let me end with a reflection on Memorial Day. Let me reflect with you on the origins of this tradition. Perhaps for a moment we can try to broaden our very definition of a battlefield. Go with me to Charleston, South Carolina at the very end of the war in 1865. Charleston, of course, was the place where the war began, a city of enormous symbolic and strategic importance. During approximately the last eight months of the war the city was bombarded by Union artillery from around the harbor and from gunboats. For many blocks up from Battery Park, some of those magnificent mansions that make that city one of the most beautiful in North America, were all but destroyed. The city was evacuated on February 18, 1865 as most of the white population fled to the interior. Among the first troops to enter the town and march up Meeting Street, the main thoroughfare of Charleston, was the 21st U. S. Colored Infantry. Their commander, Lieutenant Colonel A. G. Bennett, accepted the formal surrender of the city from the mayor.

Black Charlestonians were the bulk of the population remaining in the city in those final weeks of the war. They had witnessed death all around them for many months, and they began to plan their own rituals of mourning and celebration. On March 3 a large crowd gathered in Francis Marion Square in the heart of Charleston. Thirteen black women elegantly dressed in the finest clothes they could find and representing, they said, the thirteen original states, presented General Quincy A. Gillmore, the Union commander, with a U. S. flag, a bouquet of flowers, and a fan for Mrs. Lincoln in Washington. On March 29, African Americans in Charleston organized an elaborate parade of some 4,000 people. The march, celebrating black freedom, included two wagons (floats). The first wagon rolled along carrying an auction block and an auctioneer selling two black women and their children. The second wagon contained a coffin labeled on its side: "Death of Slavery—Sumter Dug his Grave on the 13th of April, 1861." In this mock slave auction and victory parade the freed people of Charleston declared the meaning of the war. They drew a line of demarcation between past and present. These were days of awe and wonderment, of sorrow and gaiety. The freed people of Charleston had converted Confederate ruin into their own festival of freedom.

On April 14, a celebration took place out at the mouth of the harbor in Fort Sumter itself. Four years to the day after the surrender of the fort, General Robert Anderson returned to Charleston with many northern dignitaries to raise the flag he had lowered in 1861. Three thousand African Americans crammed on to the island fortress for the ceremony. In attendance were abolitionist William Lloyd Garrison and President Lincoln's secretary, John G. Nicolay. Also among the throng were former abolitionist and writer, and now major in the Union army, Martin Delany, as was the son of Denmark Vesey, the leader of a slave rebellion who was executed in Charleston in 1822. The former slave and boat pilot, Robert Smalls, was nearby Fort Sumter aboard the *Planter* (which was filled with a contingent of freed people), the steamer he had commandeered and sailed out of Charleston to freedom during the war. The Reverend Henry Ward Beecher was orator of the day. The audience heard Beecher condemn South Carolina's secessionists to eternal damnation. Many in that special audience hoped for more guidance from Beecher about the confused and delicate questions of Reconstruction, but on that count they heard little in what unfolded as primarily a festival of victory, thanksgiving, and celebration. When hearing a regimental band play "John Brown's Body," Garrison, who two decades earlier had a price put on his life by the state of South Carolina, broke down and wept. Flowers were blooming everywhere amidst the ruins of Charleston; for so many, remembrance at this early date was but a fragrance full of warring emotions. As the flag reached its height on the staff in the fort, guns all around Charleston harbor opened up in a salute. The grand day ended that evening at a banquet in the city as Brigadier General Robert Anderson, who had surrendered the fort, among others, offered many toasts, some of which were to President Lincoln, who was that very night assassinated here in Ford's Theater in Washington. Thus the day that had begun with such jubilation ended with even greater tragedy.

During the next two weeks in Charleston, as elsewhere, mourning over Lincoln's death swept through the community of blacks and their Unionist and white abolitionist allies. Death required attention all over the land. "The dead, the dead, the dead...," as Walt Whitman lamented in one of his poems. If we really want to understand the deepest roots of reconciliation from the Civil War, it is somehow rooted in dealing with all the dead at the end of the bloody struggle. A Union quartermaster general's report shortly after Appomattox noted that only about one third of the Union dead in the war were interred in identifiable graves. The federal government instituted an elaborate program of locating and burying the Union dead all over the South in newly created national cemeteries, and by 1870, some 300,000 northern soldiers were re-interred in seventy-three national cemeteries, with 58% identified. Retrieval and recognition of the Confederate dead took much longer due to inadequate resources. Early Reconstruction policies had not extended the federal program of re-interment to Confederates. All of this death on the battlefield, as well as the deaths of thousands of soldiers in prisons, and hundreds of nameless freed people in contraband camps, presented an overwhelming psychological, spiritual, and logistical challenge of memorialization.

Charleston had more than its share of this burden. During the final year of the war, the Confederate command in the city had converted the Planters' Race Course (horse-racing track) into a prison. Union soldiers were kept in terrible conditions in the interior of the track, without tents or other coverings. At least 257 died from exposure and disease, and were hastily buried without coffins in unmarked graves behind the judge's stand of the Race Course. After the fall of the city, Charleston's blacks, many of whom had witnessed the suffering at the horse track prison, insisted on a proper burial of the Union dead. The symbolic power of the Planters' Race Course was not lost on the freed people. In conjunction with James Redpath and the missionaries and teachers among three freedmen's relief associations at work in Charleston, they planned a May Day ceremony that a *New York Tribune* correspondent called "a procession of friends and mourners as South Carolina and the United States never saw before."

The "First Decoration Day," as this event came to be recognized in some circles in the North, involved an estimated 10,000 people, most of them black former slaves. During April, twenty-eight black men from one of the local churches built a suitable enclosure for the burial ground at the Race Course. In some ten days' labor, they constructed a fence ten feet high, enclosing the burial ground, and landscaped the graves into neat rows. The wooden fence was whitewashed and an archway was built over the gate to the enclosure. On the arch, painted in black letters, the workmen inscribed "Martyrs of the Race Course." At 9 o'clock in the morning on May 1 the procession to this special cemetery began as 3,000 black school children (newly enrolled in freedmen's schools) marched around the Race Course, each with an armload of roses and singing "John Brown's Body." The children were followed by 300 black women representing the "Patriotic Association," a group organized to distribute clothing and other goods among the freed people. The women carried baskets of flowers, wreaths, and crosses to the burial ground. The "Mutual Aid Society," a benevolent association of black men, next marched in cadence around the track and into the cemetery, followed by a procession of white and black citizens. All dropped their spring blossoms on the graves in a scene recorded by a newspaper correspondent: "When all had left, the holy mounds—the tops, the sides, and the spaces between them—were one mass of flowers, not a speck of earth could be seen; and as the breeze wafted the sweet perfumes from them, outside and beyond... there were few eyes among those who knew the meaning of the ceremony that were not dim with tears of joy." While the adults marched around the graves, the children were gathered in a nearby grove, where they sang "America," "We'll Rally Around the Flag," and "The Star-Spangled Banner."

The official dedication ceremony was conducted by the ministers of all the black churches in Charleston. With prayers, the reading of biblical passages, and the singing of spirituals, black Charlestonians gave birth to an American tradition. In so doing, they declared the meaning of the war in the most public way possible—by their labor, their words, their songs, and their solemn parade of roses and lilacs and marching feet—on the old planters' Race Course. One can only guess at which passages of scripture were read at the graveside on this first Memorial Day. But among the burial rites the spirit of Leviticus, chapter 25, was surely there: "For it is the jubilee; it shall be holy unto you... in the year of this jubilee ye shall return every man unto his possession."

After the dedication, the crowds gathered at the Race Course grandstand to hear speeches by Union officers, local black ministers, and abolitionist missionaries, all chaired by James Redpath, the director of freedmen's education in the coastal region. Picnics ensued around the grounds, and in the afternoon, a full brigade of Union infantry, including the 54th Massachusetts and the 35th and 104th United States Colored Troops, marched in double column around the martyrs' graves, and held a drill on the infield of the Race Course. The war was over, and Memorial Day had been founded by African Americans in a ritual of remembrance and consecration. They had created for themselves, and for us, the Independence Day of the Second American Revolution.

According to a reminiscence written long after the fact, "several slight disturbances" occurred during the ceremonies on this first Decoration Day, as well as "much harsh talk about the event locally afterward." But a measure of how white Charlestonians suppressed this founding from memory in favor of their own creation of the practice a year later came fifty-one years afterward, when the President of the Ladies Memorial Association of Charleston received an inquiry for information about the May 1, 1865 parade. A United Daughters of the Confederacy official wanted to know if it was true that blacks and their white abolitionist friends had engaged in such a burial rite. Mrs. S. C. Beckwith responded tersely: "I regret that I was unable to gather any official information in answer to this." In southern and national memory, the first Decoration Day was nearly lost in a grand evasion.

What we need to do in Charleston in the near future is dedicate a monument to this First Decoration Day. The oval of the old Race Course is still there in Hampton Park, adjacent to the Citadel. There are many other towns that have claimed pride of place for founding Memorial Day. The good people of Columbus, Mississippi, of Petersburg, Virginia, of Waterloo, New York, and other towns are all well-intentioned in their claims for the spring of 1866. But a year earlier, African Americans did as much to create this tradition as anyone else, and they did it first.

Let me end as I began. Frederick Douglass gave us the charge for this conference, for the very ideal we meet about today, in a speech during the war. "The Mission of the War," an address Douglass gave all over the North in 1863-64, was laced with the same essential argument about the Civil War as a re-invention of the American republic as that found in Lincoln's Gettysburg Address. "A great battle lost or won," declared Douglass, "is easily described, understood, and appreciated. But the moral growth of a great nation requires reflection as well as observation to appreciate it." It was, after all, the "rebirth" of that nation that Abraham Lincoln had in mind when he spoke those words at Gettysburg about the "last full measure of devotion."

Suggestions for further reading:

Blight, David W. *Frederick Douglass's Civil War: Keeping Faith in Jubilee*. Baton Rouge: Louisiana State University Press, 1989.

_____. *Race and Reunion: The Civil War in American Memory*. Cambridge: Harvard University Press, 2001.

Davis, William C. *The Cause Lost; Myths and Realities of the Confederacy*. Lawrence: University Press of Kansas, 1996.

Dennett, John Richard. *The South As It Is, 1865-1866*. Ed. by Henry M. Christian, 1866 Reprint edition, Baton Rouge: Louisiana State University Press, 1965.

Faust, Drew Gilpin. *The Riddle of Death: Mortality and Meaning in the American Civil War*. Thirty-Fourth Fortenbaugh Memorial Lecture, Gettysburg College, 1995.

Foster, Gaines M. *Ghosts of the Confederacy: Defeat, the Lost Cause, and the Emergence of the New South*. New York: Oxford University Press, 1987.

Horwitz, Tony C. *Confederates in the Attic: Dispatches From the Unfinished Civil War*. New York: Pantheon Press, 1998.

Leonard, Thomas C. *Above the Battle: War-making in America from Appomattox to Versailles*. New York: Oxford University Press, 1978.

Linenthal, Edward Tabor and Robert M. Utley. *Sacred Ground: Americans and Their Battlefields*. Champaign-Urbana: University of Illinois Press, 1993.

Logue, Larry M. *To Appomattox and Beyond: The Civil War Soldier in War and Peace*. Chicago: Ivan R. Dee, 1996.

McConnell, Stuart. *Glorious Contentment: The Grand Army of the Republic, 1865-1900.* Chapel Hill: University of North Carolina Press, 1992.

O'Leary, Cecelia. *To Die For: The Paradox of American Patriotism.* Princeton: Princeton University Press, 1999.

Reardon, Carol. *Pickett's Charge in History and Memory.* Chapel Hill: University of North Carolina Press, 1997.

Savage, Kirk. *Standing Soldiers, Kneeling Slaves: Race, War, and Monument in Nineteenth-Century America.* Princeton: Princeton University Press, 1997.

Silber, Nina. *The Romance of Reunion: Northerners and the South, 1865-1900.* Chapel Hill: University of North Carolina Press, 1993.

Trowbridge, John T. *The South: A Tour of Its Battlefields and Ruined Cities.* 1866. Reprint edition, New York: Arno Press, 1969.

Warren, Robert Penn. *The Legacy of the Civil War.* Lincoln: University of Nebraska Press, 1988.

II. HERITAGE AND HISTORY: THE DILEMMAS OF INTERPRETATION

by Edward T. Linenthal

Being at Ford's Theater brings back many memories. My grandmother lived in Washington, D.C. when I was growing up and I used to visit Ford's Theater quite often. I think part of my enduring fascination with the Civil War and its legacy began here in my many visits. There are not many environs in which I talk, where I am in such awe. But the African Meeting House in Boston and certainly here at Ford's Theater are two places where the burden of trying to speak in ways that honor those who came before is overwhelming.

I have enjoyed, since my first visit to the Little Bighorn in 1980, a long and fruitful relationship with the National Park Service. It has been one of the great outcomes of my work on various historic sites. I have come to appreciate how important is the Park Service's work as stewards of our national memory, and how that memory has expanded beyond a narrative of war and politics to enrich our identities as Americans.

If an anthropologist from Mars would have come to the United States in 1950 or 1960 and tried to understand American history by looking at our landscape what would the anthropologist have found? Monuments, grave sites, homes of great men, great battles, and little else. Were that same anthropologist to visit today, he or she would look at a very different kind of landscape, speckled with sites having to do with women's history, labor history, as well as sites that complicate our national stories: Washita, Manzanar, Oklahoma City, and perhaps someday Wounded Knee and Sand Creek. To my mind, this is a very hopeful sign, symbolic of a nation mature enough and confident enough to engage these issues as an expression of the integrity of memory.

Now the National Park Service is called upon at a fortuitous moment to demonstrate its stewardship of integrity once again for this most profound engagement with our past, with an issue—to borrow a phrase from Robert Lowell's poem about the Shaw Memorial—an issue that "sticks like a fishbone" in our throats. I appreciate how volatile this issue is. I understand that there are different cultures in the Park Service, some resistant to change. I understand that there are regional sensitivities that will make it difficult to implement this in many ways. But the very process itself will be worthwhile. Any problematic story that stands at the center of the nation's identity will be difficult to engage. Can it, should it, be any other way? Don't we expect that Germany should agonize over proper memorials to the Holocaust? Wouldn't there be something wrong if they just whipped one out in a couple of weeks? Perhaps, as James Young says, there should never be a final solution to the German memorial question. Perhaps there will never be an end to our engagement with the issue of the Civil War and slavery, but it is our responsibility to try. How dare we ever criticize other countries—Japan, Austria, Germany—for their evasions of memory if we do not engage that which sits at the heart of American memory? If not at the sites of memory of the Civil War, where? If not the National Park Service, who? If not now, when?

Controversy over interpretation of the war, as any Civil War Park Service employee knows, is nothing new. Battlefields—Civil War or otherwise—often serve as ceremonial centers where various forms of veneration: patriotic rhetoric, monument building, preservation activities, and the ritual of battle re-enactment reflect the belief that the contemporary power and lessons of war are crucial for the life of the nation. These battle sites are more than ceremonial centers, however. They are also civic spaces where Americans of various ideological persuasion come to compete for the ownership of powerful national stories and to argue about the nature of heroism, the meaning of war, the efficacy of martial sacrifice, and the significance of preserving the patriotic landscape of the nation.

People's investment in these sites waxes and wanes with the cultural prominence of the Civil War. Interest is often sparked by major commemorative occasions or by a particular film or book or television series that captures the public's imagination about what Robert Penn Warren called America's "Homeric period." More recently, memory of the Civil War has been transformed by memories and histories of and by African Americans, perceived anew not as passive recipients of the fruits of white sacrifice, rather as agents of change who played crucial roles—North and South—in the war. Our memory of the war has been transformed by studies in the history of national memory itself, how processes of evasion, sanitization, and memorialization have too often characterized cultural responses. Cultural attitudes about the war are expressed in often bitter disagreements about the appropriate place and function of Confederate symbols: flags, songs, names of schools, textbooks, and monuments, for example. "Underlying these challenges," writes University of Mississippi historian Charles Wilson, "is the argument that the Confederacy and the Civil War had different meanings for blacks and whites and that images associated with the white past should not be used as publicly sanctioned symbols for the South as a whole." For many southern families, he observes, "the Confederacy represents not an ideology defending slavery but rather inherited stories of family danger, adherence to principle, sacrifice, and love of history. Calls to abandon these past symbols represent, to these southerners, a genealogical and cultural lobotomy."

So many issues at Civil War sites—as at other volatile sites: the Little Bighorn Battlefield National Monument, the USS Arizona Memorial at Pearl Harbor, for example—are razor's edge issues. Such controversies reveal people passionately engaged in the attempt to inscribe what they believe is the enduring legacy of the battle.

At almost any other cultural or natural history site, a call for context would be relatively innocuous. Context is defined as "the interrelated conditions in which something exists or occurs." Context provides an interpretive framework. It suggests the conceptual limits of a narrative. It situates an event in an ongoing stream of history. At natural history sites or museums, we expect to learn about the evolution of a species, or the results of archaeological work that offer a "biography" of a material resource. At a historic home, we expect our visit to be framed by stories of those who lived there, by descriptions of architectural change, or by analysis of how the evolution of domestic space reflected wider social transformations. Sites focusing on technology, music, politics all situate their stories in a context. At volatile sites, however, dilemmas abound: how can the story of the Little Bighorn be told incorporating very different experiences of Americans? Can a recent enemy be represented in the shore side visitor center at the USS Arizona Memorial without engendering accusations of physical or ideological defilement? Can Civil War sites do justice to the collected memories of Americans, "the many discrete memories," as James Young writes, "that are gathered into common memorial spaces and assigned common meaning?"

The problem, then, is not context, but continuing controversy over this context. The conviction represented in the appropriations bill certainly implies that unless slavery takes its rightful place in our Civil War narratives at National Park Service battlefields, the sites fail their interpretive charge, impoverish the intellectual and moral sensibilities of visitors, and become accomplices in continued processes of consigning to oblivion that which stood at the heart of the death struggle between the United States and the Confederate States of America. "Slavery," declared South Carolina planter William Henry Trescot, "informs all our modes of life, all our habits of thought, lies at the basis of our social existence, and of our political faith."

Some opponents of changes in substantive context argue that a site, or a monument, speaks for itself. It is enough for visitors to discern the meaning for themselves from the "facts" presented. All "facts," of course, are situated in a particular narrative and only take on meaning through them. A compilation or recitation of facts is not a narrative, but a chronicle.

I turn to one case study of memorial controversy, the Heyward Shepherd monument at Harpers Ferry, West Virginia, site of John Brown's famous raid on the night of October 17, 1859, and now a National Park Service site. This story illustrates both clashing memories of the meaning of the war and my conviction that only by telling the story—by recounting the biography of the monument—can this turbulent history come alive for visitors.

Ironically, the first casualty of Brown's raid was Heyward Shepherd, a free black man shot by one of Brown's raiders. On October 10, 1931, the dedication of a monument to Shepherd took place, part of an enduring attraction among white southerners to build monuments to so-called "faithful slaves." While Shepherd was not a slave, the United Daughters of the Confederacy adjusted the memorial message to incorporate Shepherd into the pantheon of faithful blacks who refused to join abolitionist forces. They had remained faithful to, it was supposed, those whites who knew them best and loved them. In addition to memorializing the faithfulness of such blacks, whites blessed slavery retrospectively as a system infused with civilizing, Christianizing principles, and the value of such principles was revealed in those blacks who refused to betray "their" whites.

The dedication was a remarkable event. Following speeches extolling the virtues of slavery and the wholesome world of the black "mammy," Pearl Tatten, the black music director at Storer College in Harpers Ferry arose and said "I am the daughter of a Connecticut volunteer, who wore the blue, who fought for the freedom of my people, for which John Brown struck the first blow. Today we are looking toward the future, forgetting those things of the past. We are pushing forward to a larger freedom, not in the spirit of the black mammy but in the spirit of new freedom and rising youth." No official notice was taken of her remarks, but she did receive a note from a United Daughters of the Confederacy member characterizing her comments as "untimely," and "out of place." Likewise, the *Shepherdstown Register* of October 15, 1931 reported that "her lack of propriety was severely criticized, though no reply was made to her statement nor any open notice taken of it."

There was outrage in the black community around the nation after the dedication. W.E.B. Dubois called the dedication a "proslavery dedication," and in 1932, the NAACP's Walter White asked if they might place a counter tablet on the John Brown fort—which then stood on the Storer College grounds—which would read, "here John Brown aimed at human slavery a blow that woke a guilty nation. With him fought seven slaves and sons of slaves. Over his crucified corpse marched 200,000 black soldiers and 4 million freemen singing 'John Brown's body lies a moldering in the grave but his soul goes marching on.'" The president of Storer College, fearing white displeasure, refused this request.

The monument stood relatively ignored until the National Park Service put it in storage in 1971 during major restoration work in the historic area of Harpers Ferry. The service gave assurances to the United Daughters of the Confederacy and the Sons of Confederate Veterans that it would be restored to public view when restoration work was completed. Indeed, a decade later, in 1981, the monument was restored, but the park superintendent heard rumors that it would be vandalized. He also heard dissatisfaction in the black community about the monument's renewed visibility. Consequently, he decided to put a crate around the monument. There the matter simmered until 1991, when a number of evaluative reports about NPS interpretation at Harpers Ferry suggested uncrating the monument. It was suggested that "this monument be re-dedicated and plaques installed beside the original recognizing the role and the cause of the black freedom-fighters who accompanied John Brown on his raid." In 1995, the monument was uncrated with a new interpretive plaque nearby that talked about the monument's interesting history.

The Park Service was attacked from all sides. Local representatives of the NAACP said the monument should be thrown into the Potomac—here we have the Stalinist resolution of monument problems, destroy them. Many outraged neo-Confederates accused the Park Service of "political correctness," caving in to "special interests," meaning the alleged "racism" of blacks who wanted to reinterpret the monument. For example, one critic wrote to the National Park Service superintendent, "since any monument can be considered controversial, I was wondering; is the NPS prepared to pay for a new interpretive plaque for every monument in the country that is erected on an NPS site? Is the NPS prepared to pay for the replacement of interpretive plaques as each generation reinterprets the past? Or does the concept of interpretive plaques only apply to monuments concerning black Americans? If so, does this mean that the NPS considers black Americans...to be incapable of reading historic texts, considering who wrote them and when, and then making their own judgements accordingly?"

In this letter, as in many others, there is an assertion that the monument speaks for itself; secondly, the strong reaction engendered by a very modest Park Service interpretive plaque placed near a monument which dwarfs the plaque in size is revealing. Is the objection, I wonder, to any interpretive plaque, or only one that brings into public view the vexing history of this monument, a history that complicates not only the motivation for the monument and its message, but raises important issues about the causes of the Civil War? The interpretive plaque also calls into question the very reason for erecting a monument: the desire to put in place a message that is enduring, unchangeable. An interpretive plaque declares, whatever its message, that history is not a frozen set of facts, but resembles, declared the eminent historian Carl Becker in 1935, "an unstable pattern of remembered things."

My response to this particular critical letter would point out that it is in fact the case that the Park Service is always in the process of changing interpretive programs, and often changing plaques and putting up new wayside exhibits. The service alters the contents of recorded historical messages at sites or even puts up new monuments that profoundly enrich the historic landscape, such as the Indian Memorial at the Little Bighorn. And it is clearly the case that the biography of this monument—briefly noted on the interpretive plaque—that is most revealing. The monument alone that commemorates Heyward Shepherd hides the tumultuous history of the monument's genesis, dedication, and existence, a history that reveals so much about the uses and abuses of national memory. It is also the case that those monuments that are most controversial are most in need of interpretive attention.

As with monuments, so too with battle sites. A Heritagepac e:mail alert responded to renewed interest in interpretation of slavery at Civil War battlefields by stating "battlefield interpretation should be about battles and not about subjective judgements on socio-cultural trends which happen to be politically-correct at this point in time." There is no question that many people go to battlefields to learn about the battles, and I always recall Robert Utley's caution that site interpretation must grow out of the events at the site. Given the academic world's regrettable lack of interest in military history, I understand some of the fears of those who see Civil War battlefields as among the few places where one can go and learn about, revel in, and imagine to one's heart's content the activities of individuals and armies. I can't imagine that this will ever be at risk. It is problematic, to say the least, to characterize as "trendy" the altogether defensible conviction that battles should be interpreted in the larger context of the Civil War, and situated in the larger context of what brought about the war.

I cannot see how even a cursory reading of nineteenth century evidence: political rhetoric, newspaper editorials, diaries, letters, songs, art, schoolbooks, sermons, not to mention Ordinances of Secession and the Confederate Constitution, for example, could lead to any other conclusion than that the arguments over the future of slavery was at the heart of the matter. And yet what is so self-evident to so many is read differently by others. What is central to this abiding controversy is not a disagreement over available evidence, but the difference between the sensibilities of history and heritage. "To understand something historically," Peter Novick reminds us, "is to be aware of its complexity, to have sufficient detachment to see it from multiple perspectives, to accept the ambiguities, including moral ambiguities, of protagonists' motives and behavior." Heritage, on the other hand, observes David Lowenthal, is a "felt truth," the past as we would like it to be." And, observes Lowenthal, "heroic dead are essential to the collective heritage."

Heroic dead are essential to the collective heritage. It is altogether human to resist the discomfort that comes with acknowledging that a loved one died meaninglessly, or in an unjust cause. Our urge to construct preferred narratives of sacrifice seems a constituent part of being human. I have had two recent, revealing examples of how this urge expresses itself in public. On April 19, 2000, I was in Oklahoma City for the dedication of the outdoor memorial. Before a crowd of almost 25,000 people, both Oklahoma Governor Frank Keating and President Clinton spoke of the 168 murdered as having "given" their lives. "There are places in our national landscape so scarred by freedom's sacrifice that they shape forever the soul of America," the president said. "Valley Forge, Gettysburg, Selma. This place is such sacred ground." After being immersed in the story of Oklahoma City for over three years, and coming to know well many family members and survivors, these words grated. The president tried to transform mass murder into patriotic sacrifice. It is a more comforting narrative. It situates the bombing in a long line of heroic narratives that shield us from, to use Hannah Arendt's words, what otherwise would remain an "unbearable sequence of sheer happenings."

For all the courage of family members, survivors and rescuers in Oklahoma City, and courage has been present in so many ways, these people's lives were not given in conscious sacrifice for their nation; these lives were taken in an act of mass murder. The landscape to which Oklahoma City is connected is not Valley Forge, Gettysburg, and Selma, but the 16th Street Baptist Church in Birmingham, Alabama, the McDonald's in San Diego, and Columbine High School. Listen to how the wife of a Secret Service agent murdered in the bombing responded to my question about the president's words:

> *You are right that my husband was always prepared to give his life for others. He once told me that he believed he would die young, in the line of duty. I do not think this was in any way an honorable or constructive way to die, or what any law enforcement person would choose as a way to "give" his life. Here's where my anger comes in. He was always prepared to defend the innocent, or put his life on the line to protect. He was given the opportunity to do neither in this situation. I believe we heal better when we accept the truth. This was nothing more than a damn waste of lives—all the more worthy of our heartbreak, and the families, all the more worthy of our sympathy.*

Her response, I think, is a magnificent example of the integrity of memory, of how someone seared with recent loss has the moral courage to resist the allure of preferred narratives.

And just last week, I was asked to offer summary reflections at the Center for American Studies conference at the University of Texas entitled, "To Whom Was This Sacrifice Useful? The Texas Revolution and the Narrative of Jose Enrique de la Peña." Controversy has simmered for some years about the authenticity of this diary, one of several Mexican sources which contradicts the heroic account of the combat death of Davy Crockett and several others at the Alamo. De la Peña allegedly witnessed their torture and death and pointed out how courageously they endured their fate. The alteration of a sacred story, particularly when it is part of the creation story of Texas, is a dangerous act, and vociferous condemnation greeted the 1975 translation and publication of the diary. Today, 164 years after the Alamo fell, approximately 350 people came to the conference to view a new documentary film examining the lively and ongoing battle over the diary's authenticity, and to follow eagerly a report on the ongoing scientific studies of the paper, ink, and handwriting of the diary. Were it not for the account of Crockett's death, I doubt there would have been such a conference, and had there been one, it could have been held in a small classroom.

Situating slavery at the heart of the Civil War endangers comforting notions of sacrifice as well. The "lost cause" and the strategies of reconciliation David Blight discussed offers one response. For many southerners over several generations, Confederate death could only be honorable if slavery was not the cause of the war. For many northerners over the generations, the meaning of sacrifice was not problematic because victory was theirs. The need for an honorable cause contributed mightily to the South sanitizing beyond recognition the memory of slavery. The comfort of victory contributed mightily to northern memory forgetting murderous racism expressed in, for example, the New York draft riots or the rape of freed slaves making their way to Sherman's troops in Georgia.

It is not my purpose, nor would it be appropriate, for me to tell people how to make sense of the sacrifice of their ancestors in the Civil War. What I do believe is that we honor Civil War ancestors most profoundly when we present them not as stick figures in a comforting morality play, but as complex human beings capable of all the heroism, folly, violence, and contradictory impulses that continue to define the human condition. Restoring a richer context in which these battles are described and interpreted transforms the war into more than a bloodbath. Visitors then are allowed to reflect on participants as fully human beings with convictions that might attract us, repel us, confuse us, anger us, but ultimately leave us with an appreciation for the many reasons why they fought.

"Slavery and freedom remain the keys to understanding the war," observes University of Virginia historian Edward Ayers. "Celebrating the martyrdom of whites for black freedom can reduce white guilt. Celebrating the bravery of Confederate soldiers and the brilliance of Confederate generals can trivialize the stakes of the war." Ayers calls for a "new Civil War revisionism" that would complicate the tame narratives we now employ. The war, Ayers believes, "did not have a single chronology, a rising and falling, an obvious pivot, but rather competing and intertwining chronologies in different theaters, on different home fronts, in politics and in economy.... The war seemed more pointedly about slavery in late 1863 than it did six months later when the presidential election in the North threatened to capsize the Lincoln administration. Black freedom promised more liberation in 1865 than it had delivered by 1876." A new revisionism, he hopes, might inspire accounts of battle that convey "the swirl of action and reflection, the partial knowledge of those swept up in war." Finally, he declares, "if we recognize that the Civil War did not represent the apotheosis of American ideals we might look for that culmination in the future rather than in the past."

The best interpretation at National Park Service Civil War sites already accomplishes some of what Ayers calls for. It attends to "the enduring appeals of battle," situated, however, in a larger story. And, just as attending to context resurrected the courageous voice of Pearl Tatten at Harpers Ferry—a voice silent for too long—thinking anew will no doubt give rise to voices North and South that will enrich our contribution to the enduring cultural engagement with the Civil War.

Suggestions for further reading:

Ayres, Edward. *The Valley of the Shadow: Two Communities in the Civil War.* Jefferson.village.virginia.edu (Internet publication), 1999.

Horwitz, Tony. *Confederates in the Attic: Dispatches from the Unfinished Civil War.* New York: Pantheon Press, 1998.

Linenthal, Edward T. *Changing Images of the Warrior Hero in America: A History of Popular Symbolism.* Lewiston, NY: Edwin Mellen Press, 1983.

_____ and Robert M. Utley. *Sacred Ground: Americans and Their Battlefields.* Champaign-Urbana: University of Illinois Press, 1993.

_____, et al, eds. *The Enola Gay and Other Battles of the American Past.* New York: Henry Holt, 1996.

Lowenthal, David. *The Past is a Foreign Country.* Cambridge: Cambridge University Press, 1988.

_____. *Possessed by the Past: The Heritage Crusade and Spoils of History.* New York: Free Press, 1996.

Warren, Robert Penn. *The Legacy of the Civil War.* Lincoln: University of Nebraska Press, 1998.

Wilson, Charles Reagan. *Baptized in Blood: Religion of the Lost Cause, 1865-1920.* Athens: University of Georgia Press, 1983.

Young, James E. *The Texture of Memory: Holocaust Memorials and Meaning.* New Haven: Yale University Press, 1994.

Questions and Answers for David Blight and Edward Linenthal
Moderated by Richard Rabinowitz

Richard Rabinowitz: Here is a site-specific question for David. "We read repeatedly that the healing of this nation would have fared much better if the events in this theater on April 4, 1865 had never occurred. How different would today's race relations in America be if Lincoln had survived to have a second term?"

David Blight: Thanks. The Ford's Theater question no one ever wants to have to answer. Not that much. Reconstruction surely, the politics of Reconstruction surely would have been decidedly different. Now we're beginning to play counter-factual games but that's one of the great what ifs of American history. What if Lincoln lived? Certainly the politics of Reconstruction likely would have been different. But in terms of what happened to American race relations, in terms of the ways in which reconciliation took hold in the culture by the 1870s and 1880s, the nature of the Gilded Age, economy and society, Lincoln's second term would not have much changed that. On the other hand, the violence of this event, of course, the terrible violence of this event here was a part of that pattern from the war that would sustain a certain sense of bitterness for a long time. In my book, I do actually deal with responses to the aftermath of Lincoln's assassination. I did find that fascinating. The comments and actions of many Union soldiers who were occupying sections of the South in the wake of Lincoln's death are remarkable for the ways in which they were freely willing to express their bitterness. Their hatred is tough stuff to read, but especially interesting in terms of the ways in which the American Reunion took hold in the late 19th century. I don't think Lincoln's second term could have reshaped the politics of Reconstruction, although it may have rooted black rights deeper than they were under the Johnson administration. Reconciliation of North and South well after Lincoln's presidency would still have taken the same course. I don't know if you wanted another answer to that but that's my guess. Those are good questions for which we have no evidence; we can only guess at them.

Richard Rabinowitz: Let me combine two questions for Ed. "If the bombing at Oklahoma City is not a story of sacrifice in the line of duty, but an event of the murder of innocent unsuspecting victims, do you then think it should be a National Park Service site?" Another question which is parallel, a little more argumentative. "After such an impassioned and indeed eloquent speech, mentioning images of coffins and skulls of those who fell for their beliefs, can you not affirm that the interpretation of battlefields is to reveal their sacrifice to offer the visitor a glimpse into the past when such fratricidal carnage was witnessed? To dilute such interpretation with the general primer for the public on the egregious nature of slavery is to detract from the legacy of those who fell gloriously. Do you not agree in some small part with such a contention? Those 'honored dead' are in large part why the battlefields and this very theater are preserved. Why they struggled unto death is significant, obviously, but the visitor (and I) would rather hear the How."

Edward Linenthal: Well, let me respond to that very eloquent question and comment, the second first. Of course, I think the evocative power of sacrifice at the Civil War site is part of the compelling nature of the sacred ground, but, to my mind anyway, separating the why and the how is an absolutely fatal error because it takes away the entire notion of meaning. It takes away our sense of the kinds of commitments both in terms of political causes as well as the variety of individual causes why people fought. To my mind, if a culture cannot make sense of sacrifice, if it cannot answer the why question, then that is a culture that is going to be in a tremendous amount of tension. If we look back and think about the why question, then we have to engage the fact that there were those who died fighting courageously, heroically on both sides. But certainly in the case of the Confederacy, there are many people today who are glad that the Confederacy lost. These people tend to overlook the essential fact that many of them gave their lives for a cause in which they believed. I don't see it as adding something extraneous, nor do I see this call for interpretation as detracting in any way from the power and evocation of sacrifice. So we may philosophically disagree on the function of these sites.

As to the first question, we have long ignored sites of mass murder on the national landscape. We have either resurrected them in their former state or we have obliterated them from the landscape. Oklahoma City represents a particular kind of park, something I think quite new for the Park Service—a joining together of private and public where the Park Service are stewards but not the creators of interpretive programs. This is the first site of mass murder in terms of domestic terrorism to enter into the Park Service. It is immaterial what I think about the site, because I did not have anything to do with the decision to create it. But if I had something to do with the decision, I would say the community has a right to interpret great loss however it wants, and if the Park Service believes that this is an important part of the national landscape, an important part of talking about America identity, then it absolutely should be a part of the National Park Service.

Richard Rabinowitz: I have two questions about re-enacting. They are a little different, but I think it's a subject we haven't really talked a lot about today and maybe both of our speakers would want to address this. One is: "what value does the current phenomena of Civil War re-enacting have to battlefield interpretation? Does re-enacting deepen or cheapen our sense of history?" The other one is a little different. "How can we increase the African American participation in living history interpretations? For the first two years of the war, these ill-dressed heroes risked death, capture, and slavery to perform menial camp duties. They did this service to free their fellow men and for food, freed men and contraband and dug fortifications, built pre-fabricated bridges, were cooks' helpers, photographers' aids, gravediggers, etc. Most important, teamsters could handle the tricky task of handling six mules at a time and so on.

"I do living histories at National Parks and re-enactments as the commissary sergeant of the 5th New York Duryee Zouaves. We have photos of cook's aids, and Winslow Homer painted our contraband teamsters at Yorktown. Yet, the availability of any re-enacters is nil. Indeed, the local Company B of the Massachusetts 54th Infantry is often hard pressed to come up with eight men and boys for a color guard. Perhaps the famous national spokesperson that could promote interpretation of these unsung heroes of the war of rebellion would be useful. A program for volunteers to portray their ancestors and the contributions made by them is in order but how?" So I guess the more general question is what contribution—positive or negative—is made to the interpretation of the Civil Way by re-enactment?

David Blight: Well the significance of re-enacters at battlefield sites, I would leave to you and your superintendents. In my last visit to Gettysburg (I believe it was in November or December) for a meeting there I could tell that every day of the year there are re-enacters in town. Exactly what their presence brings, I don't know, I don't live there. I'll say this about re-enacters, whatever prejudices I may have grown up with about re-enacters, I was always fascinated with these phenomena although I never have participated. Those prejudices have altered some in recent years. I edited a book of Civil War letters back eight years ago—the letters of a Massachusetts soldier from Northampton, Massachusetts. His letters were just dropped in my lap and I worked with them and published them with the University of Massachusetts Press. The press put on a little party at the Northampton Historical Society, which owned the original letters. And the re-enactment group that represented the 10th Massachusetts, which was Charles Brewster's unit, the man whose letters I edited, came out for this event—about thirty of them strong. They marched, they did maneuvers, they fired their guns, they all bought the book. Most importantly, one of them walked up afterward and said: "See this. I got Charles Brewster's Command Manual." He opened it up and there it was. "Charles Harvey Brewster," he signed it; it was his command manual that he had as a lieutenant in the real 10th Massachusetts. The re-enacter bought it at a collector's show, and there was that moment—whatever you want to call it—of authenticity, realization: "I've got Charlie's manual."

Now that was re-enactment. The other thing is that a lot of us historians at this conference in

Boston two years ago, the 100th anniversary of the Robert Gould Shaw Memorial, at which I think they had the largest gathering ever of black re-enacters—an extraordinary event. An entire session of the conference was devoted to African American re-enacters on stage describing what they do. I'll never forget the moment when one of those re-enacters got up to the podium, like this, in front of the audience, maybe even bigger than this audience today. He clicked his heels, he turned to the right, he turned to the left, and when he turned this way, his profile was amazingly like one of the men in Saint-Gaudens masterpiece, and he said: "I am the man you see in that monument." And it was one of those moments when I could realize that re-enactment is about real stuff and real feelings, and so I am very careful about what I say about re-enacters.

I was also at a conference at the Huntington Library in California last fall, attended by a whole group of re-enacters in southern California. There was a paper given that was somewhat critical of what they do. The first re-enacter got up and introduced himself as a surgeon, the next one got up and introduced himself as a lawyer, the next one got up and introduced himself as a teacher, and so forth. They were from every walk of life. They were trying to tell this particular author something about who they were—one of those moments where you had to realize re-enactments are real to the participants. So I don't know how important they are to actual battlefields, but they have become very important in the way Americans choose to remember this war.

The deepest difficulty is this problem of somehow trying to re-embody, re-enter the experience of the slave, because it resurrects all of those ugly notions of shame that are there in African American culture and have been there for decades, and decades, and surely, were there at the turn of the century in the way blacks commemorated emancipation in the War. They, themselves, engaged in a lot deflections of that slave past. It was necessary to their preferred narratives. It's a complicated problem. It's very interesting though that in this decade alone, blacks have begun to re-enact Civil War soldiers and their families on a large scale, and this apparently began particularly in response to the film *Glory*, which is yet another measure of how important films are—whatever else we might think of them.

Edward Linenthal: Just a quick comment on re-enacters—and I go back to my work on Gettysburg, which is now some years old. I really began to appreciate varieties in re-enacter culture. Before I started working on Gettysburg, I tended to place re-enacters in caricature because it's easy to do. But when I did some interviews with re-enacters, I learned about "farbs" (slang for re-enacters who need the comforts of life) and was really entranced with that whole notion. Farbs versus authentic folks—hardcore—and I thought about re-enactment as a insatiable thirst to touch, feel, and inhabit the past, which is really a religious orientation. I mean this has a lot to do with ritual and it seems to me that battle re-enactment is a particular of religious ritual.

The controversy over battle re-enactment and its function as something that may complicate our understanding of the Civil War as more than golden mist of American valor or something that really began in the centennial in the 1960s—especially when Bruce Catton begins to speak passionately against Civil War re-enactment. I don't know what's going on in how Civil War parks are interpreted, but I know it sticks in my mind from discussions with friends at Gettysburg. While battle re-enactment was famously popular at sites nearby the battlefield, certainly not on the battlefield, when the Park Service tried to do a living history exhibit of a hospital, mothers would come up and say: "Well, how dare you show my children these bloody stumps, and so forth and so on?" Well, if you're going to talk about battle, what is it in fact that you are going to talk about? So, there are some conceptual limitations to re-enactment but it seems to me also a very interesting subject. Tony Horwitz, I'm sure many of you know, deals with this at some length in *Confederates in the Attic*, a book that I very much like because there is such rich stuff in there. But it tends, to my mind anyway, to treat war as antiquarian, and human re-enactment becomes a very serious kind of issue. But there is a long history of controversy on battle re-enactment that is relevant to look at.

Richard Rabinowitz: This is a question that I think that opens up into a broader range of issues:

"When I first visited Civil War battlefields as a teenager in the 1950s and early 60s, I came thanks to my public school education, knowing that slavery was the root cause of the war and the abolition of slavery the most important result. It was obvious to me that it all related to the Civil Rights Movement of my youth. I didn't need to be told that, what I wanted to know about was what happened at the battlefield. Is today's public so abysmally ignorant of the causes and results of the war that it needs to be taught at the battlefields?" I guess I would broaden to ask of both of you as university professors and consultants on other kinds of projects to talk a little bit about where the responsibility of this education is placed in the context or the events of these battles. Where does that responsibility lie?

David Blight: Jim Horton is going to answer that one. Ignorance, yeah. Well, I mean Americans understanding of the past is what they choose to make of it all. It's done for any given citizen. I teach at a pretty elite little liberal arts college in New England. My students come from generally good high schools with good educations, but I find their historical education has become like we have become in the academy—very fragmented, bits and pieces, parts here and parts there—in many cases they don't connect events very well. They do have some notion, clearly most of my students have some notion that slavery caused the Civil War.

They know next to nothing, to be perfectly frank, about Reconstruction. I think it's still the lost history. We tend not to do summer institutes on Reconstruction. Name me a historic site about Reconstruction. We just don't treat that period as we treat the Civil War. But it's full of events, telling events. Why don't we have a national memorial to the Fourteenth Amendment? That is because it's everywhere and it's in everyday of our lives in some ways.

So ignorance is always our enemy. I assume it is in my teaching. I learned about that, I spent a year teaching in Germany as a Fulbright professor and it wasn't ignorance that I encountered from my German students. They were fascinated with the United States—at least they were in the early 1990s. There may be a little anti-Americanism setting in around the world because of globalization now and so on. They were fascinated with America but it was mostly what they knew through movies and popular culture. They have a popular culture conception of America, but what I was forced to do then is sort of slow down. I had to teach in English, slow down and develop a careful narrative of events that I had stopped doing in many ways in my own teaching. Because my audience now really needed to connect things. I tried to bring that back here, because I think my own students often need it. Whose responsibility is this? That is a huge question, Richard. It's everybody's responsibility. We are all teachers. You're (National Park Service interpreters) the front line teachers more than we are.

I still maintain the most important teaching I have ever done in my life was when I was a high school teacher for seven years. I used to take groups, busloads of fifty students from Flint, Michigan out East, as we said then, for five years in a row to Gettysburg, Antietam, and Harpers Ferry. I did a five-day tour of those sites. I had several people at those three National Parks who had become friends and my helpers in doing all of this. It was probably the best teaching I ever did because it was at sites, and I was doing it with Park Service rangers and historians. It was participatory and experiential. We're all teachers, we're all responsible for it, and we're all public historians. There is a prejudice in the academy, to be perfectly frank, about this business of public history. We're always concerned about our methods and we should be, that matters at tenure time, usually. But it's the history that's out there in the minds of the people walking the streets that matters most. Everybody has some sense of history and if we don't give it to them, somebody else will, so we're all teachers and we're all responsible for it. I have sort of been dragged kicking and screaming sometimes into the realm of public history, because I didn't always know what to do by some of my colleagues who are in this room. I'm damn glad they did.

Edward Linenthal: I mentioned at dinner last night to Jim Horton and David that I had a methodology once but it was shot off quite some time ago. But I put some cream on the area so it's a lot better now. Look, you folks know as well if not better than we, where the public is in terms of what they know about history. We have captive audiences and they have to read books because they have to take exams and they define themselves in certain ways. What I think is of real interest, where all of us have a role to play, is appreciating history not as this frozen set of facts that are sort of stored away. Ira Berlin talked today about slavery as a historical process that changes over time. Isn't one of the wonderful things that we can do at places like battlefields is talk about these places, places that have histories, that reveal our cultural engagement in a whole variety of ways? These are archives of memory in all kinds of ways. They are not only battlefields where a battle took place; they are also battlefields of memories that reveal a lot, about who we are as Americans.

I read you those wonderful words of Carl Becker, sounding very much like a so-called—dare I use the term—revisionist historian, writing in 1935 that history is an unstable pattern of remembered things. It seems to me if we can help people appreciate this, then every generation will ask questions anew of the past, engage the past in different ways, uncover new voices, and resurrect voices that have been lost. That will be a tremendous step. We have a job to do in the classroom in the area and you have a job to do on the front lines in that area. That is to my mind a tremendous conceptual challenge.

I want to pick up a point I think that's explicit in the last couple of comments. If the visitor is indeed deficient in prior knowledge coming into the park, what is the visitor most deficient in, what part of the story does the visitor know most about or less about. If we focus on right obliques, left obliques, battlefield tactics, or on the specifications of ordinance, is it because we believe the visitors are more or less knowledgeable about those issues, than about the broader contextual issues. So, I think it's an interesting argument that if the visitor is more knowledgeable about the broader issues, we may not see this as our responsibility, because people are supposed to know this from outside. So, what we are teaching in many parks may be things that in fact are so detailed and so complex that they provide extraordinarily high threshold for the ordinary visitor. Visitors have to become very interested in technical issues in order to engage the material presented by the parks.

Richard Rabinowitz: I want to look at the set of questions here that deal with our attitude toward the people of the past, so I'll read these two together. They are different but they can be joined. "The text of this message, presented today seems to be that it is time that the role of slavery in the genesis and the conduct of the Civil War be interpreted. Fair enough. Today's subtext, however, seems to be that the interpretation of slavery needs to be condemnatory of everyone who did not adopt an early twenty-first century attitude of outrage toward this 'peculiar institution.' How does the Park Service propose to ensure that the people of the past, including slaveholders and their supporters, are presented on their terms and not on ours?" That's one question, the second question, which is coming at this in another way. "Can the Confederate battle flag used outside the context of the battlefield be likened to the swastika as an icon whose meaning has changed over time?"

Edward Linenthal: I really, I have a dentist appointment now. Sorry, David. These are wonderfully thought-provoking questions, and setting the humor aside, I take this very seriously. I don't think it is very helpful to talk in the same breath about the Confederate flag and the swastika, unless we were talking generally about the volatile symbols. I don't see how linking these together is helpful. Confederates were not Nazis. Nazis were not Confederates. The flag issues that are erupting in so many places reveal how potent a symbol it is, however, and it seems to me that those who argue that Confederate symbolism was used as part of the racist reaction to the Civil Rights movement are absolutely correct. Reading Dan Carter's *Politics of Rage*, his fine biography of George Wallace, helps one appreciate how important Confederate symbolism was to whites who opposed the Civil Rights movement, often violently.

As a historic symbol, of course, the flag is part of our nation's history, and needs to be displayed in museums, and certainly in living history or battle re-enactments. Continuing to give it prominence above a state capitol, however, seems to convey that the fundamental truth of the Confederacy, that

African Americans were inferior beings, is still an operative concept in the public policy of a city, state, or nation. Here the flag does become a racist symbol. There is a wonderful discussion about various possibilities regarding Confederate symbols in Sanford Levinson's *Written in Stone*. These are raging debates that will, no doubt continue for some time.

David Blight: Well, briefly I take your point. It's a very good question. How do we care about the dead? How do we take the past-ness of the past seriously? How do you take the people within the past seriously? Especially that we don't impose a set of sensibilities of our own—that's one of the principal problems we all have. We all have our prejudices and sensibilities and we sometimes impose them. In this book, I've just finished, *Race and Reunion: The Civil War in American Memory*, I have a long chapter on the "lost cause." I also have a long section near the beginning of the book, where I try to lay down the shear variety of memories that people had, and I deal at some length with white southerners experiencing total war, experiencing total devastation and complete defeat. A loss of so many loved ones, family and so on. This was the experience of trauma on a scale most Americans have never experienced. I use for example Kate Stone's magnificent diary, it's called *Broken Burn*, which was the name of her plantation in Louisiana. It's a tragic, telling, fascinating story, a diary of a southern plantation woman who loses two of her three brothers in the war and the third one comes home and he's got battle fatigue. Actually, he's got post-traumatic stress syndrome, although they didn't call it that. He can't speak much for two years. Eventually, her life revives. She finds a man to remarry and her life does go on.

In the "lost cause" chapter, I had to deal with some people that I, of course, didn't like that much. I make the centerpiece of the chapter a woman, Mildred Rutherford, who worked out of Athens, Georgia and was the Historian General of United Daughters of the Confederacy from about 1908 to 1916. She has an incredible collection of scrapbooks at the Museum of the Confederacy. If you ever want to do research on the "lost cause," that's the place to start—dozens and dozens of scrapbooks including one full with hundreds of lynching and Ku Klux Klan post cards. She was a vehemently racist woman who had enormous power. She had southern congressmen wrapped around her finger. So she was a difficult woman to deal with, but I had to treat her for who she was, a part of her time, a woman of immense political skill. She was anti-suffrage, she believed women should wear antebellum gowns and all the rest, but there she was a very political woman all over the country for her cause. There was something human and fascinating about her and I tried to capture that. We have to get inside people's lives and whenever they lived. The thing one has to do with the "lost cause," for example, by the late nineteenth century is to treat it as a matter of "truth" and "mythology." In fact, go read the first issue, just the first issue of the *Southern Historical Society Papers*, which was the organization of the Confederate veterans in the early 1870s that came together to create the Confederate history of the war. They were led by Jubal Early and just note the times they use the word "truth" in the opening introductory essay. They are about truth; truth, truth, truth, truth, and they believe it. They don't believe Yankees and northerners can ever write their history.

Now the battle flag. I don't have a lot to add. Reactions to the battle flag are always of at least two different kinds. There's the individual reaction and there is the collective or collected—Ed wants that term collected—reaction. There's the question of whether it should be representing the state. Whether it should be a symbol of officialdom of South Carolina or Mississippi or anywhere else for that matter, that's one set of questions. Should it represent the people of South Carolina in some way? Another set of questions is how individuals react. If you have personal memories of the aftermath of a lynching in the South, where Confederate flags were used, yes, it's like the swastika. Why is it any different? I mean on the other hand, if your individual experiences with the Confederate flag had mostly to do with seeing it as a patch on the shoulders of a marching band, then, that's a different kind of reaction one might have. So we have to try to figure out whether this is an individual reaction or is it a collective reaction to how it is used by the state. I wish in this country we could fold it, and put it in museums.

Richard Rabinowitz: This is a question that uses Ed's digression into the Indian experience to be provocative. "Do you believe that Little Big Horn, Washita, and Sand Creek should interpret the whole history of the Indian experience? Can that logically be performed due to limited space, time involved in interpretation for a visitor's experience and financial resources? If one's visit is to all the above-mentioned places then a repetitive theme will exist that has little to do directly with "place," making the uniqueness of those places irrelevant." I guess I would like to ask, to sort of help sharpen that question, is there a ground between the local history, the events of the site itself and the day of the battle—is there a relationship between that and context.? How can we bridge those two things or do they have to be seen as such radically alternative notions? What are the ways in which we could understand larger stories, larger narratives as having something to do with the site itself? Is that a possible approach to drawing together the various strands of this audience?

Edward Linenthal: Again, I appreciate the thoughtfulness and the articulate-ness of this question. I guess I would frame it a different way—whoever asked this. I don't see it as either/or. Again, let me go back to Robert Utley, who cautioned me once as I was waxing eloquent to him about what interpretation could be done at the Little Big Horn. He stopped and said: "remember Ed, these are going to be seasonal rangers telling these stories." He continued by saying: "remember, always, interpretation must grow out of, but not necessarily be limited to, the experience of the site." There was a caution in a 1975 Park Service directive, concerning expanding the story at the Little Big Horn, that it should not be—it was a wonderful phrase—the occasion for an interpretive jihad that recounts the entire history of the Indian-White relations. So no, I don't think you can probably do it all. I mean it's not a place where you're going to tell the story of every Native American tribe and whether they were hunters, gatherers, or whatever. But, it certainly—the Little Big Horn to my mind—is one of the great success stories of American public culture, because it's a site that the National Park Service has mindfully transformed from shrine to historic site. It has confronted the enduring truth of first interpretation. It has not been able to tell side-by-side, differing and sometimes irreconcilable stories about the Little Big Horn. It is clear when there is an interpretive talk that's being done on tactics at the Little Big Horn that you can talk about Indian culture and how they fought war and the cultural roots out of which that came. You can talk about images of honor, valor, and courage in Native American culture and among the Army in the 7th Cavalry. So, you can do meaningful kinds of context. The Little Big Horn does absolutely talk about the Little Big Horn and the roots of Indian-White conflict. The major interpretive theme at Little Big Horn is clash of cultures. That's the context. Of course, it's done uniquely. Here's an example of how it's done well. I don't see this as a zero sum game at all.

To talk about slavery as one of the great causes of the war and the kinds of interpretive risks, then what you do at individual sites can be tailored to those sites. Absolutely, the way it's done at the Little Big Horn, which is a different site from Washita, revolves around an entire different interpretive challenge than the Washita challenges. Is it a battle or a massacre? And on that answer rides a sea change of interpretation. Context is absolutely provided there as well. The story of Oklahoma City will not just begin at 9:02 a.m. on April 19th. It will talk about the milieu and the context in which this kind of violence arose and its roots in the fertile soil in American culture from which it came. All right. The essentials are there. Why can they not be there at Civil War battlefields without diminishing what in fact is there? I think and sense that this is a zero sum game that we're in fact altering, damaging, injuring, or doing violence to the story is not a problem that I think is a real problem. I hope that my response to the question makes some sense.

Richard Rabinowitz: We have two questions. I think these should be the last. They are sort of historian's questions. One says: "What effect did the Dunning School"—referring to William Dunning, he's a professor at Columbia in the early 20th century—"have on American memory of the Civil War?" And the second question is: "In regards to what caused the Civil War, when did the state's rights, not slavery, argument take hold in the South? It seems like a post-war rationalization but when did it start?"

David Blight: Now, we're in a graduate seminar. The William Dunning school of interpretation of Reconstruction was named for the historian William Dunning who taught for many years at Columbia, trained a generation—more than a generation—of scholars between 1905 and the 1930s. They wrote and re-wrote the history of Reconstruction. They laid down, deeply laid down, with full scholarly apparatus the tragic legend of Reconstruction. No question about it. What Kenneth Stamp called the tragic legend of Reconstruction was the conception of Reconstruction as a hideous mistake, as W.E.B. DuBois once called it, ironically. It was the notion that the radical Republicans took over the South, essentially colonized it, used black suffrage, the black vote to get themselves into power and to stay in power. Most Reconstruction governments, said this interpretation, were carpetbag governments run by northerners or by blacks. It was also the argument that it was a misuse of Constitutional authority by the federal government, that it was exploitation and oppression of the southern states beyond human limits.

The great hero of the Dunning school was Andrew Johnson and the great villains were Thaddeus Stevens and Charles Sumner and the other radical Republicans of the time. That is a simplification of the Dunning school. What impact did it have on Civil War memory? A tremendous impact. But it wasn't just the Dunning school. The Dunning school came along as scholarship to harness and to develop a set of ideas and assumptions. There was a set of ideas and assumptions all over American culture in search of a history. The Dunning school gave them a history and the way that argument, ultimately, really served Civil War memory (and it is still with us) is in the notion that the South lost the war. There's no question about that. They were defeated. Slavery was destroyed. But the South won Reconstruction. The Dunning school with careful scholarly apparatus supported what the "Lost Cause" ideology had been arguing in careful ways for fifteen to twenty years, and that was a kind of victory narrative about Reconstruction. The victory of Reconstruction belonged to the South and the nation's victory over this ill-begotten wrong-headed crusade for racial equality during Reconstruction. It served the ends of forgetting what Bruce Babbitt this morning referred to, the 600 black politicians who served in legislatures and in the Congress during the Reconstruction years up to about 1890—an extraordinary political achievement. An achievement Eric Foner discussed and made famous in two books.

You cannot underestimate the impact of the Dunning school. It was directly related to the impact of a film like *Birth of A Nation*. You have to see the Dunning school and the context of the broader culture at the turn of the century, in which this whole plantation legend about the contented slave has been so deeply put into our consciousness. I never fully understood this until I did a great deal of research for this book on Thomas Nelson Page, Joel Chandler Harris, and other writers. There are many imitators who created the plantation school of American fiction who were the best selling authors of the 1890s in America.

Every story Thomas Nelson Page wrote was narrated by a faithful slave in dialect, and such was the voice in the ear of the millions of readers. This voice about slavery by the 1890s was always a happy "darkie," who was loyal to his masters, always helping the Confederate soldier come home—either dead or alive—and in the end usually conducting the marriage ceremony between the white woman and the Yankee veteran. D. W. Griffith's famous film, *Birth of A Nation*, is our most notorious example of how this kind of racism made it into popular culture, but Griffith made dozens of short films before he made *Birth of A Nation*. These little ten-minute films were happy "darkie" stories. In one of them, the faithful slave is so determined not to be freed that he finds his masters will and goes out and buries it in the ground as the Yankees are coming, because he's so desperate not to be free. I laugh at that too. I make my students read some of this. They laugh at it. But they have to understand and we have to understand, that the felt history, the felt need of that era, and the Dunning School certainly served it.

When does states rights take hold in the South? I will be very quick with that. You know the story about how Kentucky never left the Union. Nothing against Kentucky here, but Kentucky never really seceded from the Union but it joined the land of the "lost cause" after the war. It would never join the Confederacy during the war, but it became Confederate after the war. Go read the *Louisville Courier Journal* in the 1870s and 1880s. If you want to read one example of the states rights theory, in two volumes, read Jefferson Davis' *Memoirs*. His defense of the Confederacy published, in the early 1880s, is a 1200 page theoretical exegesis. It's incredibly turgid and often unreadable, but it sold widely. It was a vehement defense of the Confederacy as the vessel of the legacy of the American Revolution and the compact theory of government. But the states rights theory had been well worked out by the earliest apologists for the Confederacy. One of the best early examples is E.A. Pollard's famous book, this one is only 700 pages, published in 1867, called *The Lost Cause*. The Confederacy is immediately immortalized as a political revolution for independence against the oppression of a larger, more powerful, more wealthy foe that wanted to take away its political liberty. Everybody in the Civil War, the states rights argument would go, fought for liberty. It's just that one side had superior numbers and resources.

CITIZEN SOLDIERS OF THE CIVIL WAR: WHY THEY FOUGHT

by James M. McPherson

James M. McPherson is considered one of the leading historians of the American Civil War. His book, Battle Cry of Freedom, *for which he received the Pulitzer Prize for history, is considered the finest one-volume work on that war. In his extensive studies of the war, he continually asked himself what made Pickett's men march into a maelstrom of bullets at Gettysburg, or what made the 15th New Jersey regiment face similar odds at Spotsylvania. In his own words, he wanted to understand "what made these men tick?" From hundreds of letters and diary entries, he found that soldiers on both sides fought for their side's cause and for their comrades.*

Introduced by Robert K. Sutton,
Manassas National Battlefield Park

I take many groups around Civil War battlefields. On all of those occasions, at the very places where great events happened, at some point we feel a sense of empathy with the people who carried out those events on the battlefield. There is a sense that there are ghosts who are with us as we walk around the battlefield. I can tell you, that standing up here on the stage at Ford's Theater looking up at the Presidential box, one is certainly aware of the ghosts that are with us here. The way in which a place where, in this case, a tragic event occurred can evoke a sense of direct relationship with the past. This is exactly what we are trying to evoke when we go to a Civil War battlefield or any other historical site.

Much of what I am going to talk about this evening has actually grown out of my experience of touring Civil War battlefields and trying to answer the questions of students and alumni of Princeton, as well as other groups that I have guided around these battlefields. Many of these questions have to do with the issues of the war, the causes of the war, and the consequences of the war, as well as the details of a particular battle. We've heard a great deal from the excellent talks that have occurred at this conference about the issue of slavery and how it can be incorporated into the interpretation of Civil War battlefields. I will have something to say about that this evening. But what I'm also going focus on are some of the consequences of the war and their impact on our society, even down to today and the way in which sometimes that can also be brought into the interpretation of a specific site-related battlefield.

Let me start with a quotation from none other than Mark Twain, who co-authored with Charles Dudley Warner in 1873, a book whose title gave the name to a whole age, *The Gilded Age*. In that book, Mark Twain wrote that the Civil War "uprooted institutions that were centuries old, changed the politics of a people, transformed the social life of half the country and wrought so profoundly upon the national character that the influence cannot be measured short of two or three generations." And here we are five generations later still trying to measure that impact.

Northern victory in the war did, I think, resolve two fundamental festering issues that had been unresolved by the other most formative experience in our history—the American Revolution. Those two questions were, first, whether this fragile republican experiment called the United States would survive as one nation indivisible; and second, whether the house divided would continue to endure half-slave and half-free. Both of these issues had remained open questions until 1865. Many Americans had doubted whether the republic could survive. Many European conservatives had gleefully predicted its demise. Some Americans had advocated the right of secession and periodically threatened to invoke it. Eleven states did invoke it in 1861. But since 1865, no state or region has seriously threatened secession, not even during the decade of massive resistance in the South to desegregation from 1954 to 1964. That issue was really resolved by the war, presumably for all time.

Second, before 1865, the United States, which was wont to boast of being the freest country in the world—a beacon light of liberty to the oppressed of Europe—had in fact been the largest slave-holding country in the world. This fact caused Lincoln in a famous passage in his Peoria speech in 1854 to describe slavery as a "monstrous injustice" that enables the enemies of free institutions (he meant European reactionaries), "to taunt us, with plausibility, as hypocrites." Well, since 1865 that particular monstrous injustice and hypocrisy has existed no more. As Ira Berlin pointed out this morning, slavery was definitively ended by the Civil War. There were no serious attempts to re-enslave African Americans. The Civil War did not, however, resolve the issue of race, which was one of the principal factors underlined by slavery.

In the process of preserving the Union of 1776 while purging it of slavery, the Civil War also transformed this nation. Before 1861, the words United States <u>were</u> a plural noun. The United States <u>have</u> a republican form of government. Since 1865, the United States <u>is</u> a singular noun. The United States <u>has</u> a republican form of government. The North went to war to preserve the Union. It ended by creating a nation. This transformation can be traced in Lincoln's most important wartime addresses. His first inaugural address contained the word "union" twenty times and the word "nation" not once. In Lincoln's first message to Congress on July 4, 1861, he used union thirty-two times and nation only three times. In his famous public letter to Horace Greeley of August 22, 1862, concerning slavery and the war, Lincoln spoke of the union eight times but the nation not at all. But fifteen months later in the Gettysburg Address he did not refer to the union at all but used the word nation—in that short address of 272 words—five times. In the second inaugural address, looking back over the trauma of the past four years, Lincoln spoke of one side seeking to dissolve the union in 1861 and the other side accepting the challenge of war to preserve the nation.

The decentralized antebellum republic, in which the Post Office was the only agency of national government that touched the average citizen, was transformed by the crucible of that war into a centralized nation that taxed people directly and created an internal revenue bureau to collect the taxes. It expanded the jurisdiction of federal courts, created a national currency and a federally chartered banking system, drafted men into the army, and created the Freedmen's Bureau as the first national agency for social welfare. Eleven of the first twelve amendments to the U.S. Constitution had limited the powers of the national government. Six of the next seven, starting with the thirteenth, vastly expanded the powers of the national government. The first three of these post-war amendments transformed four million slaves into citizens and voters within five years. This was the most fundamental social transformation in our history, even if the nation did backslide on part of that commitment for three generations after 1877.

The Civil War also settled another major question that had remained in dispute during the first seventy years of the republic. Which form of economy, social relations, and culture would emerge triumphant from the contest between two distinct ways of life? Would it be the southern rural agrarian plantation society dominated by a country gentry, commanding slave labor and professing values of hierarchy, deference and noblesse oblige patriarchy? Or, would it be the dynamic northern urbanizing, egalitarian, restless, free labor, commercial, and industrializing system of capitalism? The latter prevailed, of course, and after the Civil War, the northern model of free labor capitalism became the American way. The southern way of life was gone with the wind. But as we have heard today, not entirely. It lingered on in the nostalgia of the lost cause and especially in the form of racial subordination that emerged after Reconstruction and persisted until the years of the Civil War's centennial observations, the 1960s.

Edward Pollard, who was mentioned this afternoon, editor of the *Richmond Examiner* during the Civil War, foreshadowed and in a way helped to create this nostalgia and racial subordination in the two-volume work that he wrote only a few years after the war. This first real history of the Confederacy, Pollard appropriately entitled it the *Lost Cause*. There may not be an independent political South, Pollard admitted in this work, but there can be a distinct social and intellectual South. "It would be immeasurably the worse consequence of defeat in this war that the South should lose its moral and intellectual distinctiveness as a people and cease to assert its well-known superiority and civilization over the people of the North." The war may have decided in the negative the questions of slavery and Confederate independence, Pollard conceded, but, as he put it, "it did not decide Negro equality. This new cause, or rather the true question the war revived, is the supremacy of the white race," and this issue of course is still very much with us today. It helps to account, I think, for the continuing high level of interest in the Civil War and its contemporary relevance. We have heard a great deal about that today. The Confederate battle flag dispute in South Carolina, Georgia, Mississippi and elsewhere in the South is a powerful symbol of this continuing relevance. To one side the flag represents a proud, though lost, heritage. To the other it represents slavery, racism, and oppression. To one side the flag represents liberty, to the other it represents the denial of liberty. At its core, that is exactly what the Civil War was all about.

I personally became interested in the Civil War during my years in graduate school just forty miles from here at Johns Hopkins in Baltimore in the early 1960s. Those were, of course, the years of the Civil War Centennial Commemoration but that is not what attracted me to the subject. Rather, it was the Civil Rights Movement, the confrontation between the North and South, between black and white, between the federal government and southern political leaders vowing massive resistance to national law, widespread violence, federal troops being sent into the South. Martin Luther King, Jr. urged President Kennedy to issue a new emancipation proclamation on the 100th anniversary of the first one. When the president refused to do so, King proclaimed "freedom now" in the shadow of the Lincoln Memorial at the March on Washington in 1963. I was struck by the parallels between the 1960s and the 1860s, and I then made the commitment to learn about the historical roots of my own time in the sectional conflict that became America's biggest war. It was only a matter of time before my interests in the causes and results of the war developed into an interest in the motives of the three million plus soldiers and the goals they thought they were fighting for.

What really sparked this interest more than any other single factor as I mentioned at the outset were questions that students asked me while we toured Civil War battlefields like Antietam, Gettysburg, Spotsylvania, and many others. And the questions I asked myself as I visited these sites were: what made these men tick? What enabled them to go forward into a hailstorm of lead and iron as Pickett's men did at Gettysburg or the 15th New Jersey did at Spotsylvania, knowing that their chances of coming out unharmed were slim? These questions led to a broad investigation of soldier motivation, which resulted in my book *For Cause and Comrades: Why Men Fought In the Civil War.* Over a period of several years of research, my wife and I read some 25,000 or more letters from 800 soldiers, North and South, and another 250 or so soldier's diaries. These letters and diaries are an unmatched source for getting at what these men thought and did. Because there was no censorship

1863: NEWSPAPER VENDOR AND CART IN CAMP.

✳

of soldiers' letters in the Civil War as there has been in more modern wars, and because the Civil War soldiers were more literate than the armies that had fought up to that time, these sources are very enlightening.

When I began my research in these letters and diaries, I was guided in what to look for by a substantial literature on combat motivation and combat behavior of soldiers in war. Much of the work grew out of research done by American and British social scientists in World War II, which produced, among other things, a four-volume study that still provides wonderful information, published in 1949 as *The American Soldier*. And particularly relevant is Volume II, entitled *Combat and Its Aftermath*, which is a study of combat motivation and of the soldier's psychological mechanisms for coping with the fear and stress of combat. This volume addressed the questions I was often asked by students and others during battlefield tours. This study was based on questionnaires and interviews done with thousands of GI's during and after World War II. At the same time an army historian, Brigadier General S.L.A. Marshall, carried on similar research and published his findings in 1947 in the book that has become a classic—albeit controversial—entitled *Men Against Fire*. There have been many other studies of soldiers in the British and German armies as well as the American army of allied soldiers in Korea, American soldiers in Vietnam, and so on. So I had access to a fairly large body of literature about how men behave under extreme stress, and how they deal with that stress in combat.

These studies investigated the traditional assumptions about what motivates soldiers to fight, including patriotism, ideology, religion, ideals of duty and honor and manhood, a quest for glory and adventure, leadership, training and discipline, and coercion. They found that while some or all of these factors, either alone or in combination, may have been important for some soldiers, for most, the key factor was what the experts called "primary group cohesion," a kind of jargon phase. What does it mean? The soldier's primary group consists of his comrades in the squad or the platoon or the gun crew bonded by the common danger they face in battle. They become literally a band of brothers whose mutual dependence and mutual support in combat create the cohesion necessary to function as a fighting unit. The survival of each member of the group depends on the others doing their jobs. The survival of the group depends on the steadiness of each individual, so does their individual and collective self-respect. If any of them falters, is paralyzed by fear, runs away, or, to use a Korean war phrase, bugs out, or even to use a Civil War phrase, skedaddles or skulks, that person not only endangers his own and the others' survival, he also courts the contempt and ostracism of his comrades. He loses face. He loses self-respect as a man. In other words, these studies found that the compulsion of the peer group is a greater force than coercion by officers or by the state. Or as S.L.A. Marshall in *Men Against Fire* responds to his own rhetorical question: "No man wants to die. What induces him to risk his life bravely?" It's not belief in the cause. When the chips are down, "the man fights to help the man next to him. Men do not fight for a cause, but because they do not want to let their comrades down."

There is a universality about this argument. It could apply to any war or to all wars. Given the prominence of this theme in the literature about World War II and about other modern wars, it was one of the first things I looked for when I began my research. And I found a lot about it, which I think enabled me to offer some corroborative insights on the question of primary group cohesion among Civil War soldiers. Many soldiers echoed these words of enlisted men from Texas, Massachusetts, and Alabama respectively. The Texan: "We seem almost like brothers. We have suffered hardships and dangers together and are bound together by more than ordinary ties." The Massachusetts man: "I have now spent a whole year with my comrades in battle, and having been with them in all circumstances, I must say that everyone of them is as a brother to me." Or the Alabamian: "A soldier is always nearly crazy to get away from the army on furloughs, but, as a general thing, they are more anxious to get back. There is a feeling of love, a strong attachment for those with whom one has shared common dangers that is never felt for anyone else or any other circumstances."

As I suggested a moment ago, the fear of appearing to be a coward in the eyes of your buddies, the fear of fear itself, and fear of the shame of cowardice in the eyes of your peers was a very powerful motivator in Civil War armies. I think it has been a strong force in other armies as well. S.L.A. Marshall, for example, said "personal honor is the one thing that is valued more than life itself by the majority of men." That is your honor as a man among men, the shame of being known as a coward and letting your comrades down. I think the greatest part of Steven Crane's novel *The Red Badge of Courage*, is the portrayal of how a young Civil War soldier, Henry Fleming, doubts himself and fears that at the moment of truth in combat, he would run away. Of course, he did run away. But he overcame that fear. Civil War veterans thought that Crane had portrayed this accurately and brilliantly.

After reading soldiers' letters about this same issue, I believe Crane was on target. A Connecticut private for example, wrote just before his first battle: "I am so afraid I shall prove a coward. I can hardly think of anything else." Afterwards, he uttered a figurative sigh of relief in his diary and agreed that he, in fact, had passed this test. "I was a little shaky at first, but soon got used to the music." The music, of course, was shells exploding, bullets going by his head and so on. "I know that no one will say that I behaved cowardly in the least." An Ohio soldier confessed in this diary that he was shaking like a leaf before he first went into action at his first battle but he was determined nevertheless as he put it "to stand up to my duties like a man. Let the consequences be as they might, I'd rather die like a brave man than have a coward's ignominy cling around my name and live. Of all names most terrible and to be dreaded is coward." In 1864, a New York veteran of two years responded to his sister's question. She had asked him: "aren't you scared when you go into combat? Don't you want to run away?" And he replied to her: "you ask me if the thought of death does not alarm me. I will say I do not wish to die, but I have too much honor, too much courage to hold back while others are going forward." I, myself, "am as big a coward as any could be," that is, if I were alone. "But give me the bullet before the coward when all my friends and companions are going forward."

One crucial factor I think that made this motivation stronger in Civil War armies than in American armies since World War I is that, as you know, Civil War units, most of them, were geographically recruited from the same community or region. Many of the men in a regimental company in these volunteer regiments had been friends and neighbors back home. Their families knew each other. Thus, any reports of cowardice, or bugging out, or skulking on the battlefield not only would ruin a man's reputation among his comrades, but if the news reached home, it would bring disgrace to him and his family. He could never hold up his head again at home or in the army. An Ohio officer wrote to his wife about another officer from their town who had, as he put it, "proved himself a coward on the battlefield. What a stigma for men to transmit to their posterity: 'your father was a coward.'" A Pennsylvania soldier wrote to his mother that "as Will"—Will was his brother—"says he would rather hear of my being shot than of being a coward. So I will stand up to the work I have commenced." A North Carolina sergeant said, "if any man showed the white feather, he should never return to live in North Carolina." White feather was a Civil War slang expression for bugging out or running away. This relationship between the behavior of soldiers on the battlefield and the communities from which they came is something that can be pointed out in battlefield interpretation.

As I said, there is a kind of universality about this as a motivation for men not to run away in combat, but to go forward against the enemy. It would apply, I think, just about as much in other wars, not necessarily because of local recruitment and the family or the community dimension, but certainly in the primary group—the soldiers' buddies. But for the Civil War, I found that there were some special factors, not so much in what I call combat motivation, but what I would call initial motivation or sustaining motivation. The reasons they enlisted in the first place and the reasons that these volunteer armies stuck together were in considerable part the result of ideological conviction. In much of the earlier literature on Civil War soldiers, one might get the impression that such function did not exist. There is, or at least was, a common impression that most Civil War soldiers had little or no idea why they were fighting. In William Faulkner's novel, *Sartoris*, someone asked the Confederate veteran many decades after the war what the war had been about. He scratched his head and then replied: "damned if I ever did know." A few years ago, the commander of the New York branch of the Sons of Union Veterans said: "It wasn't because our fathers knew what they were fighting for that they were heroes. They didn't know what they were fighting for exactly and they fought on anyway. That's what made them heroes."

Bell Irvin Wiley, in his two classic works, *Johnny Reb* and *Billy Yank*, reflected on that theme in his discussions of soldiers' perception of the issues about which they were fighting. Wiley was writing under the influence of a lot of literature on combat motivation in World War II and in other modern wars, which argued that patriotism and ideology ranked almost last among several factors in combat motivation for World War II soldiers. Some World War II veterans agree with this, while others vigorously disagree. I watched some of the television commemorations on the 50th anniversary of D-Day in 1994, and was struck by one veteran who said that the closer he got to the beaches of Normandy the less patriotic he felt. A British officer in World War II said: "It would be foolish to imagine that the average British or American soldier was thinking that he was helping to save democracy. He never gave democracy a thought."

Well, I don't want either to challenge or reaffirm the truth of this argument about World War II soldiers. What I am concerned about is its validity with respect to Civil War soldiers. I am aware, as you are, that most soldiers in World War II and other modern wars have been draftees or long service regulars, while most Civil War soldiers were volunteers from civilian life who continued to consider themselves as citizens and voters in uniform rather than as professional soldiers. Knowing this,

I wondered whether the denial of a strong ideological conviction that studies of World War II soldiers seemed to provide would apply to Civil War soldiers. But on the other hand there was Bell Irvin Wiley and others who claimed that it did.

Jumping off the pages of many of these letters and diaries is a contradiction to this assertion about Civil War soldiers. I was really unprepared for the prevalence of ideological themes in many, obviously not all, of the letters and diaries I read of Civil War soldiers. Many of those soldiers were intensely aware of the issues at stake in the war and were passionately concerned about them. Their expressions on the issues ranged from simple but heartfelt vows of patriotism, like "I am fighting for my country," to well-informed and often quite sophisticated discussions of the Constitution, states rights, nationalism, majority rule, self-government, democracy, liberty, and slavery.

To provide some background and context for understanding this, let me remind you again that these were the most literate armies in history to that time. In 1860, 94% of whites in the North could read and write and 83% of whites in the South could read and write. They also came from the world's most democratic and highly politicized society. Their median age at the time of enlistment in 1861 or 1862 was twenty-three-and-a-half, which meant that most of them had voted in the election of 1860, the most heated and contentious election in American history, which brought out nearly 85% of the eligible electorate. These young men had come of age in the intensely passionate and polarized politics of the 1850s. This was a period when, in seven Illinois towns, thousands of people turned out for seven three-hour-long debates to hear Abraham Lincoln and Stephen A. Douglas address great national issues. This is just one example of the way in which politics, journalism and the very life of the country in the 1850s was overwhelmingly infused with the issues over which the war a few years later was fought. And these citizen soldiers continued to vote during the war, not only electing some of their officers in these volunteer regiments, but also voting in state and national elections by absentee ballot.

Americans were the world's preeminent newspaper reading people in the 19th century. As I think most of you are well aware, soldiers continued this habit during the war when they eagerly snapped up newspapers available in camp a few days after their publication from major cities such as New York and Richmond. Here are just a few examples from many I could quote to illustrate these points. A Mississippi private wrote in his diary during the winter of 1861-62 when he was stationed in Leesburg, Virginia: "Spend much time in reading daily papers and discussing the war question in general." Two years later, an Alabama officer in the trenches at Petersburg wrote to his wife "we have daily access to the Richmond papers. We spend much of our time in reading these journals and discussing the situation." A New York captain wrote home in 1864, just a couple of months before he was killed in action: "It is a very great mistake to suppose that the soldier does not think. Our soldiers are closer thinkers and reasoners than the people at home. It is the soldiers who have educated the people at home to a just perception of our duties in this contest. Every soldier knows he his fighting for his own liberty but even more for the liberty of the whole human race for all time to come."

Several units established debating societies during less active times in winter quarters. An Illinois sergeant's diary describes some of these debates in camp near Vicksburg during the winter of 1863-64, and these are just some short excerpts from several diary entries: "Took part on the affirmative of 'Resolved that the Constitutional Relations of the Rebel States Should be Fixed by Congress Only.'" Another debate, he wrote, "discussed the question of reducing Rebel States to territories." In still another, "Sergeant Rollins and Need discussed ably, the rights of the South." (As you know in a debate, somebody has to take the unpopular side.) "Sergeant Miller expanded upon the revolution of ideas."

The following winter a New York private recovering from a wound described the debating society among convalescent soldiers which discussed among other subjects the following: "Resolved that the present struggle will do more to establish and maintain a republican form of government than the Revolutionary War." This debate theme was referenced in other letters and diaries from other Union Army units. Thus, I think this suggests that one of the dominant themes in Civil War ideology was the self-conscious awareness of parallels with the generation that fought the Revolution and gave birth to the nation. Americans in both the Union and Confederacy believed themselves custodians of the legacy of the founding fathers. The crisis of 1861 to 1865 was the great test of their worthiness of that heritage. They felt that, metaphorically, the founding fathers, a generation that was almost deified by the 19th century, were looking over their shoulders to see whether they were worthy of the heritage that those founders had left them. Soldiers on both sides felt intensely this honorable burden on their shoulders, and, of course, the tragic irony, one of the tragic ironies of the Civil War, is that Confederate and Union soldiers interpreted that heritage in precisely opposite ways. In the image of the founders, Confederates professed to fight for liberty and independence from a tyrannical government. Unionists fought to preserve the nation created by the founders from what they regarded as its dismemberment, destruction, and ruin.

A Virginia officer filled letters to his mother with comparisons, as he put it, of the North's war of subjugation against the South to England's war against the American colonies. He was certain that the Confederacy, like the earlier Americans, would win what he called this "Second War for American Independence, because tyranny could not prosper in the nineteenth century against a people fighting for their homes and liberties." That's exactly what John Wilkes Booth meant when as he jumped to the floor of this stage (at Ford's Theater) and limped across it shouting to the audience, *Sic semper tyrannis*—thus always to tyrants. He was fighting for liberty just as his Confederate friends had fought for liberty. An Alabama corporal referred in his diary to the Confederacy's struggle, as he put it, "for the same principles, which fired the hearts of our ancestors in the Revolutionary struggle."

On the other side of the lines, a Wisconsin private considered what he called "this second war equally as holy as the first by which our fathers gained those liberties and privileges, which have made us a great and prosperous nation." Justifying to this wife his decision to stay in the army after a more than a year of fighting instead of accepting a medical discharge, which he could have done, a thirty-three-year-old Minnesota sergeant and father of three young children, wrote home from an army hospital where he was recovering from wounds: "My grandfather fought and risked his life to bequeath to his posterity the glorious institutions now threatened by this infernal rebellion." He continued, "it is not for you and I or us and our dear little ones alone that I was and am willing to risk the fortunes of the battlefield, but also for the sake of the country's millions who are to come after us." Many Union soldiers also echoed Lincoln's words that the Union cause represented the last best hope for the survival of republican government in the world. I found many examples of that. My favorite has remained the expression by an Irish-born soldier, a corporal in the 28th Massachusetts of the famous Irish Brigade. He was thirty-three years old, married, a carpenter. In letters to his wife in Massachusetts and to his father-in-law back in Ireland, both of whom had questioned his wisdom—even his sanity— for enlisting to fight for the black Republican Lincoln government, this soldier wrote in some exasperation, especially toward his father-in-law: "This is my country as much as the man who is born on the soil. This being the case I have as much interest in the maintenance of the integrity of the nation as any other man. This is the first test of a modern free government and the act of sustaining itself against internal enemies." This sentiment was almost an echo of a similar statement that Lincoln had made in his first message to Congress. The soldier continued: "If we fail, then the hopes of millions fall and designs and wishes of all tyrants will succeed. The old cry will be sent forth from the aristocrats of Europe that such is the common end of all Republics. Irishmen and their descendants have a stake in this nation. America is this Ireland's refuge, Ireland's last hope. Destroy this Republic and Ireland's hopes are blasted."

The convictions of Union soldiers, as well as Union leaders, often tended to focus on what seems to us as rather abstract principles—national unity, constitutional liberty, survival of the republican experiment, the principle of majority rule, and so on. Abstract principles of liberty and self-government were, of course, important in Confederate ideology as well. Many southern soldiers were able to tie these principles to the more visceral, concrete, and, I suppose, more understandable motive of defending their land and homes against the hated invader. They believed the Yankees had come south to despoil and enslave them. Hatred and revenge became an increasingly dominant motif, I found in Confederate soldiers' letters as the war went on and as suffering and destruction escalated in the South. As a Louisiana lieutenant wrote to his mother from Virginia as early as 1862: "No union can ever exist between us and the barbarous loathsome and hateful Yankees." A Texas officer told his wife to teach their children "a bitter and unrelenting hatred to the Yankee race that has invaded our country, devastated and murdered our best citizens." Osmun Latrobe of Maryland, grandson of the famous architect Benjamin Latrobe, who designed the U.S. Capitol, fought in the Confederate army as a staff officer in Longstreet's corps. At the Battle of Fredericksburg, Latrobe directed artillery fire from Marye's Heights against the attacking Union soldiers. Afterwards, he rode over the battlefield and wrote in his diary that he had, as he put it, "enjoyed the sight of hundreds of dead Yankees. Saw much of the work I had done in the way of severed limbs, decapitated bodies, and mutilated remains of all kinds, doing my soul good. Would that the whole northern army was such and I had my hand in it." Now there is naked hatred and desire for revenge.

Southerners related this hatred and revenge to more abstract ideological principles. If one word occurred more than others in Confederate ideological rhetoric, it was the word "liberty." And of course, the opposite of liberty was slavery. Southern soldiers talked of escaping enslavement to those hated Yankees. A Mississippian from a slaveholding family said he was fighting to help "drive from our soil the ruthless invader who is seeking to reduce us to abject slavery." A Georgia soldier wrote to a friend that "the deep, still quiet, peace of the grave is vastly more desirable than slavery."

Now these Confederates were using the word "slavery" in the same sense that American Revolutionists of 1776 had used it. Some of them could go on in the next sentence to assert the protection of property rights in black slaves as a reason for fighting. I think that the leaders of the revolutionary generation, Jefferson, Madison, George Mason, George Washington, and others saw considerable incongruity and felt considerable embarrassment about fighting for their own liberty while continuing to hold blacks in slavery. That sense of embarrassment and awkwardness in the revolutionary generation did not exist among most Confederates, as far as I have been able to determine. I think that a generation or more of the pro-slavery defense of the institution as a positive good had actually caused southerners of the Civil War generation to believe deep in their bones that slavery was a good. Therefore, they saw no hypocrisy, no inconsistency, no incongruity about saying they were fighting for liberty at the same time they were also fighting to preserve slavery. As a Texas officer put it that "if we lose this war," this was in 1864, "we will lose slavery, liberty and all that makes life dear." A Georgia captain who owned forty slaves, wrote to his wife in 1863 from the front in Virginia of "the Arch of Liberty we are trying to build." And several sentences later he advised her to sell a troublesome slave. Three weeks later, he reassured his wife, who had expressed doubts about the survival of slavery as an institution after the war, that if the Confederacy won the war, "slavery is established for centuries." A Georgia officer fighting in the Atlanta campaign during 1864 wrote to his wife: "In two months more we will perhaps be an independent nation or a nation of slaves. If we lose, not only will the Negroes be free but we will all be on a common level."

This equation of emancipation with black equality was common in the South. It was one of the fears that kept so many non-slaveholding whites on the firing line. One of them, a Texas private, remained confident even as late as 1864 that Confederate victory would prevent the freedom of the slaves, and that Confederates had a greater motive to fight hard than did the Yankees because, as he put it, "we are fighting for matters real and tangible, our property and our homes. They, for matters abstract and intangible for the flimsy and abstract idea that a Negro is equal to an Anglo-American." He wasn't really right about that. Relatively few Yankees professed to fight for racial equality, and, in the early part of the war, not many white Union soldiers claimed to fight solely or primarily for emancipation.

What united Union soldiers was the cause of Union. For a long time the issue of emancipation sharply divided them. There were a good many northern soldiers from early in the war who did see it as a war that linked Union with the freedom of the slaves. That produced a kind of ideological mix of liberty and union, one and inseparable. A Massachusetts private told his parents in early 1862 that he considered, as he put it, "the object of our government is one worth dying to obtain. The maintenance of our free institutions—the Union—which must of necessity result in the freedom of every human being over whom the stars and stripes wave. Who can desire peace while such an institution of slavery exists among us?"

But there were soldiers in the Union army in 1862 who felt just as strongly on the other side. And indeed, this issue badly divided Union soldiers, especially during the six or eight months surrounding the time that Lincoln issued the preliminary and the final Emancipation Proclamation during the winter of 1862-63 and helped to contribute to a severe moral crisis in union armies. A New York artillery officer wrote in 1862 "the war must be for the preservation of the Union, the putting down of armed rebellion and for that purpose only." He went on to write that if Lincoln gave in to radical pressure to make it an abolition war, "I, for one, shall be sorry that I ever lent a hand to it." In the officers' mess of a New York regiment, a lieutenant in January 1863, after the final Emancipation Proclamation was issued, took part in "several pretty spirited, I may call them hot, controversies about slavery, the emancipation edict and kindred subjects." Obviously, within his mess, there was a sharp division of opinion. "It is not a very acceptable idea to me," he wrote, "that we are Negro crusaders." But then, interestingly enough, he concluded, "anything, as I often said, to crush the rebellion and give us back the Union with all its stars would be desirable."

This last sentence, I think, provides a key to understanding a significant change that occurred in the Union army after about mid-1863. One can trace the turning point to the victories at Gettysburg and Vicksburg. Up until that time, defeatism and incompetent leadership and the idea that the soldiers were risking their lives to free the slaves had contributed to a severe morale crisis in the Union armies. After the victories at Gettysburg and Vicksburg, with the accompanying sense of elation, that sentiment radically changed and the degree of anti-emancipation grousing, dissent, and disaffection in the Union armies sharply declined. Many soldiers previously opposed to emancipation came to accept it—not so much as an ideological war aim—but rather as a means to weaken the Confederacy by taking black manpower and bringing it over to the side of the Union. One of the best examples of this was a colonel from Ohio, Marcus Spiegel. He came from a Democratic background, and in January 1863 he wrote to his wife: "I am sick of this war and I do not find a want to fight for Lincoln's Negro proclamation any longer." Only a year later, shortly before he was killed in the Red River Campaign in Louisiana, this colonel who had been in Louisiana now for several months, told his wife "I have learned and seen more of what the horrors of slavery was then I ever knew before. I am now a strong abolitionist." I think as most of you are aware, when Lincoln ran for re-election in 1864 on a platform that pledged a thirteenth Amendment to the Constitution to abolish slavery forever, which provided the sharpest contrast between the Republicans and the Democrats in that election, he received nearly 80% of the soldier vote.

These two themes of soldier motivation—patriotism and ideological conviction, on one side and primary group cohesion or solidarity with your buddies as a second motivation—are the "cause and comrades" in the title of my book. In discussing these themes, I also distinguish between what I call sustaining motivation and combat motivation. Ideological conviction was a crucial component of sustaining motivation. That was the glue that kept these largely volunteer armies together through the hardest and most dangerous soldiering Americans have ever done. Solidarity with your buddies, the fear of appearing a coward in their eyes and those of friends and family at home, were the principal factors in combat motivation—the courage that enabled men to go forward in that hail of bullets. In my book, I try to tie these two factors together. There would not have been fighting soldiers and cohesive armies without both a commitment to the cause and a commitment to your comrades. And when I take students and other groups around Civil War battlefields where these very questions and motivations first surfaced with me, I also try to tie together both of these factors. In turn, I try to link them to the larger themes, that I discussed at the beginning of the lecture, in order to place that particular battle in its context of the war as a whole and that war in its larger context of American history.

Questions and Answers:

Question: Do you believe that Lee's aggressive offensive strategy, which was very costly in lives lost, ultimately led to the defeat of the Confederacy?

Answer: During the 1990s, there has been a major debate among military historians concerning Lee's offensive strategy, that was very expensive in terms of casualties for the Confederate army. As a number of historians have been arguing in recent years—there are a half dozen books that make this case now—Lee adopted the wrong kind of strategy for the Confederacy. In short, this argument states that Lee's strategy cost them a great deal in casualties rather than conserving their limited manpower. They further suggest that the Confederates should have adopted a strategy something like George Washington did in the American Revolution to keep the army together, minimize casualties, be less aggressive, and not fight a battle unless there was a reasonable chance of winning it.

I am more inclined to agree with the people who challenge that idea; principally, I agree with Gary Gallagher who has spoken on and written a great deal about it. Yes, while Lee's strategy was expensive in terms of casualties, Lee is the one commander who won a lot of battles and came close on more than one occasion to winning the war. He was also nearly successful in convincing the northern people that they could never overcome the rebellion. That this happened in 1862, again in 1863, and even in 1864 when he was fighting on the defensive because he no longer had a choice but to do so. Lee was the one Confederate commander whose success nearly won the war. Here, winning meant that he was close to discouraging the North from trying to conquer and subdue the South and destroy its armies.

Many who criticize Lee's strategy point to Joseph Johnston as the finest Confederate strategist. Johnston adopted the Fabian* strategy of protecting his army, preserving it for another day, and avoiding a battle in which he might lose everything. That Johnston lost Vicksburg, might have lost Richmond in 1862 if he hadn't been wounded, and to a large degree was responsible for the ultimate loss of Atlanta does not speak well for his strategy. Certainly, Jefferson Davis looked upon Johnston as being responsible for these defeats and he thought that Lee's strategy had a real possibility for winning the war. Thus, I am inclined to agree with Gary Gallagher. I know far less about the Confederate strategy and leadership than he does or a lot of others do, but I have been persuaded by that argument.

Question: Do the United Daughters of the Confederacy and the Sons of Confederate Veterans have a positive role to play in American life today or do they stand for white supremacy? And, do you think the Confederate flag has a place in military parks?

Answer: I would like to take the second part of that question first. I think the Confederate flag does have the place in the museums of military parks because it is an artifact of Civil War battlefields. The controversy is about the battle flag and not the Confederate national flag, so the context in which it has a genuine legitimacy and relevance is in a battlefield context.

As far as the United Daughters of the Confederacy and the Sons of the Confederate Veterans, I

---

* The term Fabian is derived from the Roman commander Quintus Fabius Maximus. In the year 217 BC, Fabius delayed the defeat of Rome by Hannibal and the Cartheginians by dogging the footsteps of his enemy, cutting off foraging parties, and avoiding a major battle. Fabius' tactics were unpopular in Rome and earned him the nickname 'Cunctator,' which meant delayer.

was a strong supporter of the Sons of the Confederate Veterans effort to erect a statue of General James Longstreet. I agreed with the North Carolina Chapter of the Sons of Confederate Veterans slogan that "it's about time." I lent my support to that effort and gave them some money, and now that one and only monument to General Longstreet is at Gettysburg. I think that has been a positive contribution. I think they have made other positive contributions. The United Daughters of the Confederacy are playing an effective role in the creation of the National Park Service's Soldiers and Sailors database. So, yes I do think that they can play a constructive role helping to understand all sides of this highly controversial and highly divisive issue of what the Civil War was all about.

Question: What direct role did slaves play in battles?

Answer: In many of the battles, they did not play a direct role as soldiers but they did play an important role on both sides in the early parts of the war with their labor power, especially with the Confederacy. Antietam offers an easy example. The limited Union victory at Antietam provided the occasion for Lincoln to issue the Emancipation Proclamation. It is easy to interpret slavery and black troops at Petersburg at the Crater, for example, or at other parts of the Petersburg battlefield because black troops fought there. This would be true on other battlefields as well. Some of these sites are managed by the National Park Service and some are not.

But how would one interpret slavery or the contributions of African Americans at Kennesaw Mountain? Well, who dug all the trenches and the elaborate fortifications that Johnston set up as he retreated southward from Rocky Face Ridge to the outskirts of Atlanta in the spring and summer of 1864? Every one of those defensive positions including the ones at Kennesaw Mountain had been prepared in advance by slave labor impressed or conscripted into the Confederate Army. Slave labor was crucial as teamsters, as laborers, as cooks, sometimes as musicians, as nurses, and in every other way you can imagine. Body servants accompanied most Confederate officers, thus there is a story for any battlefield. And as is well known, as the war went on, the Union army came to rely increasingly on contraband slave labor to do much of the work. They, for the most part, did not dig trenches, although they did in some instances, but they served as teamsters, as laborers, as cooks, and any number of other capacities. Without them, both armies would not have been able to function. Of course, in the latter part of the war at many battlefields there were black soldiers on the Union side.

I think the issue of slavery and race can be presented in many different ways. At Gettysburg, for example, in a kind of way that may not appear very obvious, there was a fairly sizeable free black community. There were several free black farmers who had small farms on the land that is now part of the Gettysburg National Military Park. The most familiar one is the Bryan House right near the High-water mark. Well, where were all those blacks when the Confederates came to Gettysburg? They had all taken off. They had fled because they feared they might be captured and sent south into slavery because they heard well-founded rumors and stories that as the rebels came north they did seize those they claimed escaped from slavery from Virginia and Maryland. Well, that's a way to interpret the issue of slavery at Gettysburg. There are many different ways if you carefully and conscientiously dig into the relationship between slavery, freedom, black labor and black soldiers in the war. These stories can be included in almost any of the battlefield parks.

Question: For the past two decades, I have been either with or connected with the National Park Service. Implementation of this Congressional mandate is the first time in my memory I have seen such a productive alliance between the agency and academia. Do you see an integration of academic historians and the interpretative process continuing or coming to an end when the mandate has been satisfied?

Answer: I see it continuing. I hope it will continue. I think conferences like this are one way of continuing it. Several years ago the Organization of American Historians, which is the leading professional association of academic historians who write about history of the United States, worked out an agreement with the National Park Service for evaluation of their interpretation at all of the historical sites. I was on the visiting committee for Gettysburg. That is a relationship that I look forward to continuing, as the Gettysburg National Military Park continues the process of interpreting the battle in its new visitor center and putting the battle into the larger context of the issues of the war such as we have been talking about in this conference. I think that is a relationship that should continue. I have long been an advocate of the responsibility of academic historians to a larger constituency than their colleagues and their students. Their responsibility to the public sphere is a wonderful way for academic historians to contribute their knowledge and expertise. So, I look forward personally to a long, and I hope productive and cooperative relationship with the National Park Service. I hope that many of my other colleagues will do so as well.

Question: What can you tell us about the white southerners who remained loyal to the Union and actually fought in the Union army?

Answer: Richard Current who wrote a book about eight years ago called *Lincoln's Loyalists*, discussed precisely this subject. Many who read Current's book were a bit surprised. Counting West Virginia, which of course was part of Virginia when the war started, close to 100,000 whites from Confederate states fought in the Union army. Most were from Tennessee—some 40,000 to 50,000—and the next largest number came from West Virginia. But as you suggest, from every Confederate state, except South Carolina, there was at least a battalion or regiment of whites who fought in the Union army. Yet there is very little known about this and I do not know whether there are any monuments in West Virginia or East Tennessee to these loyalists.

How do you interpret that? Well that's a good question. I think that issue ought to be interpreted at the parks where it's relevant. Chickamauga and Chattanooga would be a good example. In the Atlanta Campaign there were many white Tennessee regiments in those operations. It raises the question of the concepts of unionism, of loyalty, of nationalism, and the way in which the Civil War is commemorated and remembered in the South.

Suggestions for further reading:

Catton, Bruce. *Mr. Lincoln's War*. Garden City: Doubleday, 1951.

_____. *Glory Road*. Garden City: Doubleday, 1952.

_____. *The Stillness at Appomattox*. Garden City: Doubleday, 1957.

Daniel, Larry S. *Soldiering in the Army of Tennessee: A Portrait of Life in a Confederate Army*. Chapel Hill: University of North Carolina Press, 1991.

Davis, William C. *Lincoln's Men: How President Lincoln Became a Father to the Army of the Potomac*. New York: Free Press, 1999.

Dean, Eric T. *Shook Over Hell: Post Traumatic Stress, Vietnam, and the Civil War*. Cambridge: Harvard University Press, 1999.

Frank, Joseph Allan. *With Ballot and Bayonet: The Political Socialization of American Civil War Soldiers*. Athens: University of Georgia Press, 1998.

Glatthaar, Joseph. *The March to the Sea and Beyond: Sherman's Troops in the Savannah and Carolina Ï*

Hess, Earl J. *Liberty, Virtue, and Progress: Northerners and Their War for the Union*. New York: Fordham University Press, 1997.

_____. *The Union Soldier in Battle*. Lawrence: University Press of Kansas, 1997.

Jimerson, Randall C. *The Private Civil War: Popular Thought During the Sectional Conflict*. Baton Rouge: Louisiana State University Press, 1994.

McPherson, James M. *For Cause and Comrades*. New York: Oxford University Press, 1997.

Mitchell, Reid. *Civil War Soldiers*. New York: Penguin Press, 1997

_____. *The Vacant Chair: The Northern Soldier Leaves Home*. New York: Oxford University Press, 1995.

Power, Tracy J. *Lee's Miserables: Life in the Army of Northern Virginia from the Wilderness to Appomattox*.

Chapel Hill: University of North Carolina Press, 1998.

Robertson, James I., Jr. *Soldiers Blue and Gray.* Columbia: University of South Carolina Press, 1998.

Wiley, Bell Irvin. *The Life of Billy Yank: The Common Soldier in the Union.* Baton Rouge: Louisiana State University Press, 1979.

_____. *The Life of Johnny Reb: The Common Soldier in the Confederacy.* Baton Rouge: Louisiana State University Press, 1989.

✳

HANDBILL: FEBRUARY 27, 1837.

OUTRAGE.

Fellow Citizens,

AN

ABOLITIONIST,

of the most revolting character is among you, exciting the feelings of the North against the South. A seditious Lecture is to be delivered

THIS EVENING,

at 7 o'clock, at the Presbyterian Church in Cannon-street. You are requested to attend and unite in putting down and silencing by peaceable means this tool of evil and fanaticism. Let the rights of the States guaranteed by the Constitution be protected.

Feb. 27, 1837.   *The Union forever!*

SLAVERY AND THE COMING OF THE CIVIL WAR: A MATTER FOR INTERPRETATION

by James Oliver Horton

What caused the Civil War? Was it the institution of slavery? Was it states rights? Or, was it something else? Professor James Oliver Horton looks at what contemporaries had to say on the subject. He quotes from soldiers—officers and enlisted men—from political leaders, and from African Americans. His evidence is convincing, and should leave absolutely no doubt what caused the Civil War.

Introduced by Dwight Pitcaithley,
Chief Historian, National Park Service

This morning I want to talk about the centrality of the institution of slavery to the interpretation of battle sites and the Civil War. In the late 1980s, I taught at the University of Munich and I found teaching in Germany very, very instructive. Sometimes when you teach abroad you learn much more than you teach. Last fall, I published a book entitled *Von Benin nach Baltimore: Geschichte der African Americans.* I say that so you can appreciate my accent and multi-lingual abilities. This is a book on African American history, written in German, and published in Hamburg, Germany. As you may have guessed, the book is co-authored and one of the authors is a German native speaker, a professor of American history from Hamburg.

We published this book to address the intense interest in African American history that we observed all over Europe. My German students were interested in all kinds of things about African Americans in the United States, but they were really interested in the institution of slavery. What was it? Why was it? How could it be? What did it do? What did it mean? What is its legacy? They were so interested, that I began to wonder why. Obviously, slavery was not particularly important in Germany. After much discussion it became clear. As one student explained, "this is one of the evils we were not responsible for." Growing up in this generation, one can understand the difficulty many German young people have talking about their own national history. There is an attractiveness of a history of another country, which, in many ways, they find as shameful as they find parts of their own. So, I want to talk about the institution of slavery, as it is central to American society and to American culture.

The centrality of this institution to America and to American identity is older than the nation itself. Even today, in debates about flying the Confederate flag over the state house in Columbia, South Carolina, or at football games at the University of Mississippi, or as we discuss Virginia's official celebration of Confederate History during the month of April, we cannot escape the meaning and the consequences of slavery, that great contradiction to our most sacred national principles.

First, I want to remind you of just how important that institution of slavery was to our national history in the years before 1860. By 1815, slavery was the most important labor system that produced the most valuable export—cotton—of the entire nation. And by 1840, cotton was more valuable than all other U.S. exports combined. By 1860, the value of southern slaves was greater that that of all of America's factories, railroads, and banks put together. Sometimes we talk about slavery as if it were a side show to American history. It wasn't. It very decidedly was the main event. Do this: look through the *Congressional Globe* (the *Congressional Record* of the early 1800s). There, you will find more debates about slavery than any other single issue in our national Congress in the years before the Civil War.

I want to set this institution of slavery at the center of the war. And, I want to argue that—here it is straight and as plainly as I can say it—slavery was the central cause of the Civil War. Others have said it and I want to say it very plainly. I want to be clear because when you say things like that, people hear all kinds of other things. So, let me tell you some things I am not saying. I am not saying that slavery was the only cause of the Civil War. I am not saying that slavery was the stated reason for Abraham Lincoln declaring war. And, I am not saying that slavery provided the personal reasons for every individual in the United States or the Confederate armies for taking up arms, although James McPherson has clearly shown that many soldiers on both sides of the battle line left no doubt that they were in this fight because of this institution of slavery. What I am saying is this: the protection of slavery was the foundation that moved the South toward secession, and it was the underlying reason that the Confederacy was formed. Confederates were willing to take up arms against the United States of America in order to preserve the institution of slavery. More importantly, from the standpoint of many slaveholders and non-slaveholders—especially non-slaveholders in the South—they were passionate to preserve the way of life that slavery made possible.

Almost all academic historians and many public historians have long accepted the fact that slavery was the primary cause of the Civil War. But, as National Park Service historians and historical interpreters go about their duties of teaching about the Civil War, and you really do a great deal of teaching about the Civil War, you know better than I, that you are likely to encounter strong opinions to the contrary. National Park Service historians and historical interpreters have faced notable reaction when they have attempted to place slavery at the center of the war. John Latschar, the Superintendent at Gettysburg National Military Park, can tell you about the reaction that he received when he, as an aside, mentioned that slavery was one of the causes of the war. Eleven hundred people wrote to the Secretary of the Interior demanding his resignation. We, in the academy, almost never have to face this kind of reaction. Clearly, to discuss slavery in this context is to strike at a raw nerve among many who seek to celebrate the bravery of their ancestors who fought for the Confederacy. It is obviously easier in the twenty-first century to celebrate the southern cause of states rights or to focus on the tension of two opposing economic systems, than it is to focus on slavery as the war's central cause. But, whatever the reasons we debate in the twenty-first century, the fact remains that in the middle of the nineteenth century it was clear to most Americans that the Confederacy was formed and warred against the United States of America over the question of slavery. It was just that simple; and it is not simple at all.

Today, we talk about revisionist history as if it were a new and dangerous thing. In reality, every generation revises its history. We should feel no more threatened by revisionist history than we would by revisionist medicine. The practice of medicine during the time of the Civil War did not understand, treat, or guard against infection. Is that the kind of medicine we want to provide for our loved ones at the beginning of the twenty-first century? Of course it is not. The fact is that revising history is what historians are supposed to do. Historians who are not constantly trying to revise history are not doing their jobs, and can be replaced by a simple tape recorder. In some ways, the move away from the notion of slavery as the central cause of the Civil War was itself a kind of irresponsible revisionist history. Nineteenth century people recognized that slavery was very much a central cause of the conflict. There are plenty of primary sources that make this claim irrefutable. Let me quote from some of this plentiful evidence this morning. I think it is important to use primary source of material, because standing out in a battlefield in the middle of a hot summer day, with kids screaming, tourists in shorts and fanny-packs, you are on the spot and need to know a great deal about what you are telling the public. You need to have evidence. The only defense you have is knowledge. So, if you want to feel as comfortable talking about slavery as a part of the Civil War as you are talking about the maneuvers on the battlefields or the furnishings in the historic houses, you need solid evidence.

Let me give you some examples of the kinds of evidence that will make your argument persuasive to people—even to people who do not want to hear it. As I said earlier, in the middle of the nineteenth century, almost all Americans agreed that slavery was the central cause of the war. Certainly, African Americans believed from the beginning that if the United States won this Civil War, slavery would be destroyed. "From the first," said Frederick Douglass, "I, for one, saw this war as the end of slavery, and truth requires me to say that my interests in the success of the North was largely due to this belief." Blacks understood that slavery could not be abolished within the framework of the United States Constitution as long as the Southern states remained a major force in the federal government. Slaveholders could block any potential amendment that could end slavery. Since the Constitution protected private property, Congress was virtually powerless to pass any legislation that might cripple or ultimately abolish the institution of slavery. War was the surest, and perhaps the only way to destroy the institution of slavery at that moment.

There was great optimism among African Americans on hearing of the South's intention to secede. In his message to the South, black abolitionist Charles Lenox Remond left no doubt as to his feelings about secession. "Stand not on ceremony, go at once," he said. African American men had formed military units throughout the northern states during the 1850s. They had been training, they had been waiting for the opportunity, as one put it, "to strike a final blow for freedom." They saw the Civil War as the continuation, and hopefully the completion of the American Revolution. They hoped that the Civil War would give them access to the freedom promised during revolutionary times.

But, Abraham Lincoln initially refused to enlist blacks in the federal army. In an effort to hold the loyalty of the Border States, which were also slaveholding states, Lincoln announced that the war aim was the salvation of the Union, not the destruction of slavery. It was clear at the start of the war that the United States did not intend to abolish slavery in the South. Lincoln did not intend to interfere with slavery in places where it existed. In fact, he even offered to support a constitutional amendment, which ironically would have been the Thirteenth Amendment, to guarantee the right of slaveholders to hold slaves forever. As Eric Foner told us thirty years ago, the Republican Party's call for free soil, free labor, and free men focused on the western territories, not on the slaveholding South. In 1861, the abolition of slavery was not an issue that most white Americans in the northern states were willing to go to war over.

Yet, most northerners were concerned about slavery. They were interested in restricting slavery's expansion to the West—the place of America's future. They wanted to reserve America's future for free white labor. Said differently, at the beginning, this war was about slavery, but not simply a struggle between the abolitionist North and the pro-slavery South. In the South, things were quite different. From the very beginning, most southern leaders saw the coming of the war as one important means of protecting and preserving the institution of slavery. Let me tell you what they said. Alexander Stephens of Georgia, future Vice-President of the Confederacy understood what the South was fighting for long before the war came. A decade before secession in reaction to the debate over the Compromise of 1850, he wrote to his brother Linton. "The great question of the permanence of slavery in the southern states," he said, "was critical to maintaining the union." Then, as if

KING COTTON.

to anticipate William Seward's irrepressible conflict speech eight years later, Stephens predicted "that the crisis of that question [that is the slavery question] is not far ahead." He said this in 1850. The Compromise of 1850, especially the Fugitive Slave Law which was part of the Compromise, was designed to assure the South, but it was not enough to allay southern fears. As abolitionists continued to resist, the South remained skeptical of federal resolve to enforce the Fugitive Slave Law. Despite his guarantees, after Lincoln was elected to the Presidency in 1860, most southern whites agreed with whites from South Carolina, that when he came into power, he would "foment a war that would be waged against slavery until that institution shall cease throughout the United States."

South Carolina's fears for the safety of its peculiar institution, which is what slavery was often called, led its leaders to call for a convention in Charleston just before Christmas in 1860. At this convention, they declared that the "Union heretofore, existing between the State of South Carolina and the other states of North America is dissolved." The reason for this drastic action, South Carolina delegates explained in their declaration of causes for the secession, was what they termed a broken compact between the federal government and slaveholding states. The non-slaveholding states had refused to enforce the Fugitive Slave Law.

Let me pause here for a moment. Southerners were saying that part of the reason that South Carolina was seceding from the United States was because the federal government was not enforcing federal law—the Fugitive Slave Law. Think about this for a second. How does this concern comport with the argument that the southern effort to protect states rights was the cause of the Civil War? In the late 1840s and the 1850s, Massachusetts, Pennsylvania, other northern states passed laws called personal liberty laws. These personal liberty laws made it illegal for state representatives and state facilities to be used for the capture and return of fugitive slaves. The Fugitive Slave Law, a national law, overrode these state laws. Therefore, South Carolina should have stood solidly in opposition to the Fugitive Slave Law, for it violated the principle of states rights.

The Fugitive Slave Law was the immediate cause of the Civil War according to a number of southern states. Georgia seceded less than a month after South Carolina. Its governor, Joseph Brown, explained why Georgia seceded. He said that Lincoln was "a mere instrument of the great triumphant party [the Republican party], the principles of which are deadly hostile," not to states rights, not to tariffs, not to internal taxes, but "deadly hostile to the institution of slavery." One Georgia editorial confirmed what most white Georgians and most white southerners believed: "Negro slavery is the South and the South is Negro slavery." This is what they meant when they talked about the southern way of life. Editorial opinion in the *Augusta Daily Constitution* agreed: "our ideal is a pro-slavery republic," it said. When Alabama seceded, it sent Robert Hardy Smith to the provisional Confederate States Congress. In that body, Representative Smith set out the reasons why his state was leaving the United States. "The question of Negro slavery," he made clear, "has been the apple of discord in the government of the United States since its foundation." On this point, I agree completely with Representative Smith. Slavery was indeed the central divisive issue over which the Union had been broken, and I quote him again: "we have dissolved the late Union chiefly because of the Negro quarrel."

These quotes are pretty straightforward. But to leave no doubt about the link between secession and the institution of slavery, on March 21, 1861 in Savannah, Alexander Stephens, then Vice President of the Confederacy drew applause when he proclaimed: "our new government was founded, its foundations are laid, [and] its cornerstone rests upon the great truth that the Negro is not equal to the white man. That slavery, submission to a superior race, is his natural and normal condition. This is our new government," Alexander Stephens said. "It is the first in the history of the world based on this great physical, philosophical and moral truth." I find these statements convincing. Those in power in the South understood that their withdrawal from the United States was directly connected to the protection and preservation of their institution of slavery.

But, you may have questions. These quotes certainly raise questions for me. Only 25% of the people in South owned slaves. How about the other 75%? Why did 75% of the people in the South, who held no slaves, go to war to protect slavery? Again, let's turn to the record. Let the South speak for itself. *The Kentucky Statesman*, a newspaper in Lexington, warned its readers about the dangers of allowing any split between slave owners and non-slave holders. The newspaper contended that this was "the great lever by which the abolitionists hope to extirpate slavery in the states. Southerners must be careful not to fall victim to the propaganda that sought to raise suspicions that the non-slave holders would not stand for slavery." In reality, the newspaper argued, "the strongest pro-slavery men in this state are those who do not own one dollar in slave profit." The editors encouraged those who doubted this to "travel to the mountainous regions of the state," where one would find "thousands of as true southern men as tread the soil of cotton states with comparatively few slave owners among them." Significantly, pro-slavery men were equated with true southern men, for slavery was the essence of southern society. The newspaper contended that slave owners and non-slave owners alike "believe slavery to be right and socially beneficial." "The interest felt by non-slaveholders of the South in this question is not prompted by dollars and cents," the newspaper said, "but by a loyalty to the southern way of life."

There was a special issue of the *Louisville Daily Courier* with an even more direct message to non-slaveholders. The abolition of slavery, it argued, would elevate African Americans "to the level of the white race and the poorest whites would be closest to the former slaves in both social and physical distance." Then came the most penetrating question that cut to the core of southern racial fears. "Do they [non-slaveholders] wish to send their children to schools in which Negro children in the vicinity are taught? Do they wish to give the Negro the right to appear in the witness box and testify against them?" Finally, the article moved to the most emotionally charged question of all. Would the non-slaveholders of the South be content to live with what the writer contended in bold, upper case letters, was the ultimate end of abolition, "TO AMALGAMATE TOGETHER THE TWO RACES IN VIOLATION OF GOD'S WILL." The conclusion was inevitable the article argued. Non-slaveholders had a real stake in the maintenance of slavery. Everything that they could do, they should do, to maintain its presence. African American slaves were the only things that stood between the poorest whites and the bottom of southern society. And if they fell to the bottom of southern society, they would share that space with black people.

These arguments were extremely effective—even the poorest white southerners got the message. Their interest in slavery was more important than simple economics. As one Southern prisoner explained to his Wisconsin-born Union guard, "you Yankees want us to marry our daughters to niggers." This fear of the loss of racial status was common. A poor white farmer from North Carolina explained that he would never stop fighting because what he considered to be an abolitionist federal government was trying "to force us to live as a colored race." And, although, he had grown tired of fighting, a Confederate artilleryman from Louisiana agreed that he must continue to fight because he would "never want to see the day when a Negro was placed on an equality with a white person." These non-slaveholders surely recognized their stake in the institution of slavery and thus their stake in this war.

Most Confederates would have agreed with the assessment of the southern cause set forth by a Union soldier in 1863. Shortly after the passage of the Emancipation Proclamation, he wrote, "I know enough about the southern spirit that I think they would fight for the institution of slavery even to extermination." Lincoln's issuance of the Emancipation Proclamation in 1863 transformed this war into a holy crusade against slavery, but there was never complete agreement among federal troops about outright abolition. Yet, increasingly after 1863, as James McPherson tells us, pro-emancipation conviction did predominate among the leaders and the fighting soldiers of the United States army. Nevertheless, United States soldiers, whether they were fighting to limit slavery or fighting to abolish slavery, the focus was on the institution of slavery, as it was in the South.

A half-century after serving in the Confederate cause, John Singleton Mosby, leader of Mosby's Rangers—the Gray Ghost—offered no apologies for his southern loyalties and he was quite candid about what he was fighting for. "The South went to war on account of slavery," he said. "South Carolina went to war as she said in her secession proclamation, because slavery would not be secure under Lincoln," he continued. Then he added as if to dispel all doubt, and as if speaking directly to us today, "don't you think South Carolina ought to know why it went to war?" Of course, Mosby was right. South Carolina did know why it went to war. South Carolina knew exactly why it seceded. South Carolina, Georgia, Mississippi, Louisiana and the other southern states, one by one, at the time of their secession and all through that war told us over and over again it was about slavery. Why don't we believe them?

It is hard for us at the beginning of the twenty-first century to think about secession or slavery as a cause of the Civil War, not because of what happened then, but because of how we view what happened then. There should be no confusion, based on the fact that a wide variety of southerners, from private citizens to top governmental officials, from low ranking enlisted men to Confederate military leaders of the highest ranks, and from local politicians to regional newspaper editors, all agreed that slavery was the central cause of the Civil War. Perhaps the denial of that fact has something to do with race. Slavery has been over since 1865, but the legacy of slavery remains very much with us today. This is the context within which we have to function.

David Blight writes in his forthcoming book *Race and Reunion*, that national reconciliation after the Civil War was brought about in large part by a kind of unwritten agreement between the northern states and southern states. The North was willing to let the South handle the issue of race and even supported the system of Jim Crow in exchange for getting on with the Union and the industrial revolution. I would argue that the North and the South both paid a price for that agreement, but it is obvious that African American people in the North and the South paid the greatest price. They continue to pay that price today in order that the nation can imagine itself as a place united in a commitment to freedom and equality. This is the context within which your conversations in battlefields take place. This is part of the reason why conversations on these issues are so tough.

Last weekend I attended a conference New York City held in conjunction with an exhibit at the New York Historical Society entitled "Without Sanctuary." The exhibit focused on lynching, and its impact was stunning. I have studied many horrifying moments and events in American history including slavery, the middle passage, and some of the bloodiest race riots imaginable, but nothing prepared me for the sobering effect of confronting the reality of lynching. The exhibit was based on a collection of post cards. People took pictures of lynchings, put them on postcards, and sent them to their friends through the mail. The images of black bodies hanging from trees or engulfed in flames were unspeakably horrible, but what affected me most were the white faces in the crowd. We tend to think of lynching as something that happens in the deep dark woods, hidden away from public view, but obviously this was not always true. Some of these lynchings were announced in advance in local newspapers and attracted thousands of people—10,000 came to a lynching in Memphis. They came by chartered train, from out-of-state, with picnic lunches. Some brought their children. And yes, there is a connection between that exhibit and what we are talking about today. The symbols of the Confederacy were prominent in the crowd. The faces of the children and the adults showed that they were enjoying the spectacle as they waved Confederate flags and wore rebel caps. There was a pathology there, a pathology shaped over generations as a significant aspect of American culture.

When you approach the notion of slavery as a cause of a war a hundred or more years ago, keep in mind that that part of our past is not totally past. The Civil War was about slavery and as we discuss the Civil War we do so in a time that is all about race. Again, your job in talking to the public about these uncomfortable issues is not an enviable one. Yet, your job is critically important. National Park Service historians and interpreters will educate more people in the course of a month than I will in a lifetime. That makes what you do both difficult and vital. I have always been amazed to watch interpreters do what they do under the most inhospitable of circumstances. What you do is central to education in this country. As Thomas Jefferson believed, an educated electorate is democracy's best safeguard. You are democracy's "safeguarders." You do the critical work of educating the nation's future generations. I take some heart because I have always been impressed with the seriousness with which you approach your work. We need that seriousness, and we need for you to educate yourselves so that you feel comfortable enough to say the tough things that need to be said in the places where most people come to learn American history.

Questions and Answers

Question: Most interpreters are, perhaps, not opposed to the incorporation of slavery into their interpretations of Civil War battles on its face. However, the question is how to do so without making that incorporation seem out of place, or cheesy, as it were, to the specific battle, rather than to the war as a whole?

Answer: That is a very good question. Again, the more you know the easier it is to do this. It becomes obvious if you are interpreting Antietam. Antietam, of course, is intimately attached to the institution of slavery in that it was the vehicle for the announcement of the preliminary and final Emancipation Proclamation. So, there are places where slavery is closely attached to the site and the war. But, it is hard to think of some place where slavery could not be interpreted, although there are places where slavery is more central than other places. One of the things that maybe I should have said is this: I am not saying that slavery is of equal import in every single situation, of course not. But there are important situations throughout the war in which slavery was essential, and those are the places where you can use your interpretive skills to make the visitor aware of that.

Let me give you an example of what I am saying. A couple of years ago, I was talking to a person who had a plantation to interpret, with slave quarters out in back. But, he wanted to focus on the house. He did some interpretation of slave quarters out in back, but, since people really wanted to come into the house, how, he wondered, could he interpret slavery in the house. The question I asked was very simple. Who built the house? Further, there were only a few white people living in the big house, but on a day-to-day basis on a large plantation black people would have been most in evidence. An unknowing stranger visiting Monticello in 1790 might well have believed himself to be in a black neighborhood. It makes about as much sense to interpret a plantation simply from the point of view of the slaveholding family, as it does to interpret Harlem simply from the standpoint of the area's white business owners. In both cases the vast majority of the people were people of African ancestry. Therefore, if you heard a person singing, if you saw a person walking, if you saw a person wearing clothes in a particular way, if you saw a cultural celebration going on, it was likely to have been influenced by the majority of the people in that place.

Keeping these simple and obvious things in mind, makes your job a lot easier. Interpreting slavery means more than just looking at the place of particular slaves, at this spot, at this time, doing this thing. Southern society, in fact much of American society in the eighteenth and nineteenth centuries, was built around and shaped by the presence of that institution. People generally do not think about how widespread the impact of slavery was, and not only in the South. Go north to Brown University in Rhode Island for example. You may think you've escaped slavery's influence, but you have not. Rhode Island was one of those places in the North that had some of the region's largest plantations—called estates—but really they were plantations. The Browns were slaveholders, but more importantly, from an economic standpoint, they also were large-scale slave traders. It is very difficult to go any place in this country, especially in the eastern part of this country, and not run face to face with the impact of slavery. Again, the more you know the easier it is for you to do that.

Question: While southern secession was unquestionably about preserving slavery, was the war? Since the burden of prosecuting the war was to restore the Union as the United States Government's and Lincoln's stated aim, rather than to abolish slavery, it seems clear that while the political crises that led to the war was slavery, the actual shooting and killing was about something very different, federal supremacy. In truly understanding the war isn't it necessary to separate the two?

Answer: Let me tell you a story. There were some drug dealers and they had the drugs in a house. Before the police came, they were focused on the drugs. When the police came, they lost focus on the drugs and started shooting at the police. Am I telling a story about anti-police action or am I telling you a story about the protection of drugs? The fact is that the political situation that led to the war would not have occurred in that way if there had been no institution of slavery.

It would be interesting to do a poll asking this question to the people in South Carolina in 1860. If you were absolutely certain that the federal government would in a constitutional amendment protect the institution of slavery, would you be willing to sacrifice your young men to fight against the federal government to lower the tariff? I think they would not answer in the affirmative, especially given the economic importance of cotton as the raw material purchased in large quantity by northern dealers for textile manufacturing. If you remove the South's perceived need to protect slavery from this equation you don't have a Civil War at this point. I cannot imagine people saying well, I think I'll just get up and take up arms against my country because of some vague economic abstraction like the tariff. And remember, when South Carolina threatened nullification over the tariff in the early 1830s, not a single other southern state was willing to follow its lead. The fact is that slavery was the central issue of the politics that led to the military conflict. If you remove that central issue from the politics, you remove that which leads to the war. So I am not sure I can answer that question except to say no, I don't think so.

Question: What would you say to a visitor who would contradict the issue of slavery as the cause of the war?

Answer: I would ask what was the cause. What do you think the cause was? It does seem to me that it is your responsibility to be able to take on those kinds of questions. I always say this to students, if you have an opinion and you present your evidence and someone presents counter evidence that you can't explain or overcome, then you have to reassess your opinion. A good historian can never ignore counter evidence. That is the difference between history and propaganda.

So, you have to listen to what they have to say, you have to take their argument seriously, and theoretically, you should be able to explain why, despite what their argument might be. Now the problem as I understand it is when and how to do this. I, as a professor, have less of a problem because I can say "Okay, fine. Let's sit down and talk about this. Let's break up into groups in the room." Or we can talk individually, or we will talk about this next time we are together, or we'll read some things and come back and talk about it. You don't have that luxury. In some ways that makes the job harder and it makes the job more important. You need to be able to talk about their arguments directly, so if they give you some of the most common issues— it's about states rights, it's about different economic systems, it's about tariff control—you can be prepared and answer their questions. Now there is always a possibility that somebody is going to come up with an argument that you have never heard before in your life. I can't tell you what to do there. The best you can do to draw on the knowledge that you have to answer the argument the best you can, or just say you don't know. But, as I say to my students who are studying for graduate oral exams, if you have read widely and thought carefully about your subject, only on rare occasions will you encounter a question for which you are totally unprepared. But there is real pressure to do your homework in great detail.

The last thing, and this is something you already know, and this is the most important thing about what you do, which is as you talk to one person, you know there are many other people listening.

Many of those people listening are going to be or maybe have been in situations where they were asked that exact question and they didn't have an answer. They are looking to you to provide them with an answer for the next time they're asked that question. That really puts on the pressure. But again, take the question seriously enough to construct an answer. I would try to take the argument straight-on and answer the question. That is part of the reason why in my talk I wanted to answer some of the issues that are generally raised, states rights, and so on. Because I know those are the kinds of issues that you will be faced with and it's hard to do this with all those people watching you and time pressure. But of course that's why they pay you the big bucks!

Question: Didn't the authors of this country's constitution see the hypocrisy in the phrase "all men are created equal?" Is it because they did not recognize people in bondage as human beings but property/chattel?

Answer: Well, it is certainly true that some people did recognize the hypocrisy. Abigail Adams wrote to her husband, John, saying it was confusing and hypocritical that "we are daily denying from others that which we are demanding for ourselves." Benjamin Rush, thought slavery and liberty in one society were hypocritical. Incidentally, lots of slaves thought it was hypocrisy too, and they said so in petitions to the federal government and to state governments. They called on America to do what America said it was about. "We expect great things," they said, "from men who have made such a noble stand against the designs of their fellow men to enslave them." I generally get this question when talking about Thomas Jefferson because people say he was just a man of his time, when everybody believed as he did that slavery was justifiable. The fact is that everybody did not. Benjamin Franklin, Alexander Hamilton, John Jay were among those who led antislavery societies during that time. It is certainly true that the argument that justified slavery placed emphasis on the inferiority of black people. In fact, in some ways, the argument that justified slavery is our greatest nemesis in the twenty-first century.

We were a society coming into being on the slogans of freedom and liberty. In some ways it might have been better for slaves had we not been a society based on the ideal of freedom. Suppose we had made the argument that we were holding people in slavery because we had the power to do it. We have the guns, the whips, and the chains, and we will hold people in slavery as long as we have power and they do not. In some ways that would have been better because when those in power no longer had the guns, whips and chains, the burden of slavery would have been over for the former slaves. But, because we were a society that wanted to think of itself as a freedom-loving society, as a society committed to human rights, as a society committed to morality, as a Christian society, we had to find some justification for holding people in bondage that didn't contradict this image. But because we wanted to see ourselves in those terms, we had to invent theories about black people being racially fit for slavery. It's not us, it's not that we would use power in inhumane ways, it's that they, those Africans, have something about them that makes it okay for us to enslave them. In fact, white Americans argued that black people were better off in slavery. Slaveholding, some whites claimed, was their Christian duty. America was developing the theory of white supremacy, and Thomas Jefferson was very much a part of this. Things that we now think of under the term racism were used constantly to defend the institution of slavery. Now here is the big problem for our society today. Slavery was ended in 1865, but the racism that rationalized it is still with us. The hypocrisy of rationalization remained through the 20th century. It was used to justify Jim Crow, to justify lynching, to justify a variety of things that happen in today's society—things that may be more obscure but have the same racial rationalization.

Foundations for our views that justified racism certainly were there before the American Revolution. But there was an important change that took place. There was a time in the eighteenth century when—although race was always important—class played a much more important role than we would think, when comparing it to the middle of the nineteenth century. For example, in 1740-

41 in the slave conspiracy to burn New York City, whites and Native Americans were executed for their roles. When seamen rioted against impressment in the 1750s and 60s, these were black seamen and white seamen. When crowds rioted against British taxation and the Stamp Act in the 1760s there were blacks as well as whites. It was no accident that, Crispus Attucks, a free black man, led the mob at the Boston Massacre in 1770. John Adams defended the British soldiers who killed Crispus Attucks and others in that mob. When he recounted the event he explained that the Americans were led by a fugitive slave of Native American and African parentage. But John Adams was not shocked that this was an interracial mob. He wasn't because it was not surprising. Many, if not most of those pre-revolutionary mobs were interracial. It is significant that the revolution itself was fought on both sides with interracial units, the last time the American armed forces fought in integrated units until the Korean War. Race was becoming the central divider of Americans at the end of the eighteenth and into the early years of the nineteenth century while slavery was being justified to a greater and greater extent on issues of race. That is the background for the coming of the Civil War and for what Civil War soldiers referred to as the southern way of life.

Question: Do you think the Civil War was an irrepressible conflict?

Answer: What if Nat Turner had been successful? What if John Brown had been successful? What if the railroad had not been established? What if the canals had not been built? What if the major economic relationships had remained in the Midwest between the North and the South? What if the Midwest and the South had been united economically against the Northeast? Under those conditions, would there have been a Civil War, or, if there had been a Civil War, what would have been the sides? Nothing is ever inevitable. But you can see at particular points, looking back from this vantage point, that if that had happened a little differently things might have been different. I would never argue for the inevitability of the Civil War, because even up to the very end when John Crittenden was trying for a big compromise that Lincoln was willing to support, the war might have been forestalled. The war could have occurred at a variety of points before. What if South Carolina had not stood alone in the nullification crises of the early 1830s? I suppose I would argue that it is not possible to answer that question. I guess I would ask what is the value of posing the question, because ostensibly what you are saying is that you can isolate this single thing in history. I don't think that you can. Certainly, by the 1850s, if I were betting person, I would be betting on the Civil War. By the 1850s I think you have a good shot at winning your money because I think as you go farther along your odds get better and better and better, that there is going to be a Civil War. Alexander Stephens predicted it in 1850. I think he would have been really safe in predicting war after Kansas-Nebraska and probably a foregone conclusion after John Brown. Stranger things have happened. Here's one. Suppose Henry Clay had been alive in 1860-1861. Would he have been able to craft a new, binding compromise? I don't know.

Question: Without the Civil War [and if the war had ended within the first twelve to sixteen months] might slavery have lasted into the 20th century?

Answer: That is an excellent question. I actually have done a lot thinking about this and talking to students about this. Slavery was never a static institution. It was constantly changing. Look at slavery in the seventeenth century, look at slavery again in the middle of the eighteenth century, and look at slavery again in the middle of nineteenth century. You see different institutions. Look at slavery in the northern part of the South, in Virginia or in Maryland and compare it to slavery in Mississippi, Louisiana—the Delta area—you see very important differences in the institution. Perhaps slavery would have remained, but it would have changed. The Tredegar Iron Works used slave labor in manufacturing. People said slaves would never work in those kinds of factory situations. Either they did not have enough mental capacity to handle the complicated machines, or they would sabotage all those machines and blow the factory up. Well they were trying it very successfully in the Tredegar

Iron Works. So what does that tell us? Maybe you would have a kind of evolution of slavery toward manufacturing. Don't forget that 10% of the slaves were working in non-agricultural work—lumber and sea trades—as well as in small factories.

They were doing a variety of things. So, since there are many possibilities for changing slavery you could say slavery would have existed but it would have changed. At what point does change become so great that slavery no longer exists? I do not have the answer to that question either. But again, when you pose these kinds of questions you have to be aware of their complexity. The former slaves probably would not have stood for the country returning to business as usual when the war was over. There were many slaves who walked off the plantation and officially or unofficially found sanctuary behind federal lines. Some African American abolitionists speculated that maybe we should not have fought a Civil War in the first place. If the South formed its own nation with four million captives, without the protection of the full force of the United States Government to hold those captives in place, they thought that John Brown's raid would not have been the last. The fact is that there were many possibilities for the way things might have been different had the war either not come or not moved as it did. But again, whenever you ask these kinds of questions always be aware of the complexity of the question that may not be readily apparent unless you think a great deal about the context. Thus context, in reference to the battlefields, is so important because it does help you to think in a more complex manner and more deeply about the possibilities.

Question: How do we incorporate broadly fashioned interpretive programs on the issue of slavery into our battlefield parks?

Answer: The obvious answer to that is that we need to talk about the reason that the battlefield existed in the first place. Let's face it; that piece of land was there long before the battle, and it would still be there, but you would not be there. And so, one straightforward thing you can say is that the reason we are here is because this battle took place within this context. When you say that, of course, people have a right to know why people would be willing to give their lives in this place. The answer to that leads directly to this issue of slavery. Again, I would not say that slavery could be equally interpreted in every place. But when you're talking about the Civil War, it is hard to think of places where slavery has no place. The other thing I think you can do is to give the visitor a sense of the time, not of this time, but of that time. What was life like? Why did it make sense for this particular person, this soldier, to be at this particular place? What was the world of this soldier like—the world that would bring him to this spot? Now, I think you will find that visitors will really appreciate trying to imagine what life was like at some distant point in the past. And as you do that, for the middle nineteenth century, slavery becomes an important issue.

The point is not that you should talk about slavery simply to talk about slavery. You want to talk about the things that help you to understand the historical significance of a particular time and place. It just so happens that when we are talking about the Civil War and the central issues of that war, we are talking about a time when slavery was so very influential. That is the reason, not because it is politically correct to do so. But, it is historically correct to talk about the institution of slavery when you're talking about the Civil War. Beyond that, I think, if you use the basic philosophy that these are the issues that set this place into context, it allows us to understand the historical significance of a particular place. So long as you approach the subject that way, I don't think you will have very much trouble finding ways to fit the institution of slavery into your basic interpretation. This is not a matter of whether we want slavery to be important in the Civil War; it was.

It is hot and humid in Washington, D.C. in the summertime. Regardless of how we feel about it, uncomfortable summers are reality in the nation's capital. By the same token, it doesn't matter what we think, it doesn't matter what we want, and the fact is that slavery was a central part of the Civil War. Now, we can make several decisions. We can say okay, it was but I am not talking about it. You can do that but you can't wish it away. It was there. If you accept that fact, it becomes easier for you to understand that since the institution of slavery was an important part of these historical events, it fits naturally into your interpretation. I think it is harder to rationalize not including the entire story, because sooner or later somebody is going to ask you a really embarrassing question. The fact is that slavery was there. Slavery was important. You have the responsibility of interpreting the history, and since slavery is so much an important part of that history, it becomes part of your responsibility.

Suggestions for further reading:

Barney, William L. *Flawed Victory: A New Perspective on the Civil War.* Lanham, Maryland: University Press of America, 1980.

Boritt, Gabor S., ed. *Why the Civil War Came.* New York: Oxford University Press, 1997.

Davis, William C. *The Cause Lost : Myths and Realities of the Confederacy.* Lawrence: University Press of Kansas, 1996.

Foner, Eric. *Free Soil, Free Labor, Free Men: The Ideology of the Republican Party Before the Civil War.* New York: Oxford University Press, 1995.

Faust, Drew Gilpin. *The Creation of Confederate Nationalism: Ideology and Identity in the Civil War South.* Baton Rouge: Louisiana State University Press, 1990.

Freehling, William W. *Prelude to Civil War: The Nullification Controversy in South Carolina, 1816-1836.* New York: Oxford University Press, 1992.

_____. and Craig M.Simpson, eds. *Secession Debated: Georgia's Showdown in 1860.* New York: Oxford University Press, 1992.

Horton, James Oliver and Lois E. Horton. *In Hope of Liberty: Culture, Community, and Protest Among Northern Free Blacks, 1700-1860.* New York: Oxford University Press, 1996.

Levine, Bruce. *Half Slave and Half Free: The Roots of Civil War.* New York: The Noonday Press, 1992.

McPherson, James M. *For Cause and Comrades: Why Men Fought in the Civil War.* New York: Oxford University Press, 1997.

_____. "The Heart of the Matter," *New York Review of Books* (October, 23, 1997), 35-36, 46-47.

Rozwenc, Edwin C. and Wayne A. Frederick. *Slavery and the Breakdown of the American Consensus.* Boston: D. C. Heath, 1964.

Wakelyn, Jon L. ed. *Southern Pamphlets on Secession, November 1860-April 1861.* Chapel Hill: University of North Carolina Press, 1996.

THE CIVIL WAR HOMEFRONT

by Drew Gilpin Faust

What was it like to be a plantation wife in the South during the Civil War? What was it like to be a northern wife? With a high percentage of the men from both sides away at war, and with a shortage of available staples, the lives of those left behind often were quite difficult. Professor Faust has been at the forefront of the scholarship on the Civil War homefront, and more particularly how the war affected women. Not surprisingly, she finds that their lives were very difficult. But she also found that most women bore their new burdens, and came out of the conflict saying, as did one Confederate woman, that it was "certainly our [war] as well as that of the men."

Introduced by Mary Ann Peckham
Stones River National Battlefield

In the past decade, the Civil War home front has attracted new and significant attention. The almost exclusive focus on military history that prevailed in writing about the war had yielded only a few explorations of the lives of civilians, and many of these studies had focused on politics and the public arena. The growing importance of social history in the 1970s and 80s affected almost every area of the study of the American past before finally in the late 1980s its practitioners began to direct their attention to the almost unparalleled riches of the Civil War era—the extensive collections of official records as well as the letters and diaries often produced by individuals who never would have recorded their experiences for posterity apart from the crisis of war. The arrival of social history in Civil War studies has transformed the field—in its military as well as nonmilitary dimensions. Much of the best recent writing on soldiers has focused on the everyday lives of common infantrymen, on the texture and meaning of their experience. But social history has also encouraged scholars to look beyond battle, at the world behind the lines, at the experiences of civilians white and black, male and female, as they found themselves caught up in the maelstrom of war.

It is on the lives of such individuals that I would like to focus my remarks today. "Home front" is a bit of an amorphous category and might be seen to include such non-military dimensions of the war as Union and Confederate politics, finance and economic policy. But instead of examining these public dimensions of civilian life, I would like to explore what we have learned about the everyday experiences of the ordinary men and women across the nation who were also significant actors in the drama of Civil War.

It is important at the outset to emphasize that there was no single Civil War "home front"—no single experience that can encompass the variety of civilian life between 1861 and 1865. North and South, Union and Confederacy endured the war quite differently—primarily because of the far greater pressure the war placed on the economic and manpower resources of the South. A far higher percentage of Confederate than Yankee men left their homes and jobs and families to serve in the army: four out of five white southern men of military age entered the army; fewer than half of northern men did so. And a far higher percentage of Confederate men died in military service, leaving a greater proportion of widowed, orphaned and bereaved southerners. The death rate—numbers of deaths in comparison to the size of the population—was 6% in the North and a striking 18% in the South. As a South Carolinian observed in 1863, "death has been in our midst as a people."

Even within North and South, different "home fronts" existed. Those portions of the Confederacy subjected to military invasion became a realm not easily characterized as either home or battlefront, and these areas incurred particularly high costs during the war. Families living in much of Virginia, for example, endured the presence of troops and the loss of their crops, livestock and property to the military for four long years. Their war was very different from that experienced by individuals remote from the line of battle. These sorts of contrasts were less important in the North, for only a few areas confronted actual Confederate military invasion. Nevertheless, the war had a different impact on city dwellers and rural residents. Even within the same geographic areas North and South, wars' effects were different for rich and poor, black and white, women and men. This attention to difference, to the complexity of the civilian experience, and to the kinds of conflicts that occurred behind the lines has been a major contribution of the new social history to our understanding of the Civil War.

Historians have been particularly assiduous in exploring these divisions within the South—possibly because such investigations seemed to offer a means of using social history to answer one of the central and abiding questions of Civil War historiography: why the Confederacy lost. An older portrait of a patriotic and united white South has yielded to an understanding of the Confederacy as plagued by conflict. The war's economic demands and the departure of nearly a million white men from productive labor into the military created hardships keenly felt by yeoman and planter families alike. Shortages of food—probably the result of inadequate distribution systems rather than actual absolute shortfalls—plagued many soldiers' wives and children. Cloth production was imperilled both by absence of raw materials and by the Confederacy's inability to manufacture the cotton cards essential for home clothing manufacture. A Georgia grand jury proclaimed in August 1862, "We are grieved and appalled at the distress which threatens our people especially the widows and orphans and wives and children of our poor soldiers." An official in Alabama noted that in parts of the state citizens were actually dying of starvation.

Many desperate southerners blamed these hardships on the rich and powerful, manifesting a sensitivity to class differences that had been muted in the general prosperity of the white South in the 1850s. Accusations of "extortion" against merchants and other individuals believed to be hoarding necessities became a central theme of Confederate public discourse. Both the Confederate government and individual states endeavored to respond to this discontent, both with largely ineffective laws against price gouging and with unprecedented efforts to provide direct aid. In some areas of North Carolina, for example, as many as 40% of white women received government support to relieve hunger and deprivation.

Historians differ on the question of how effective these welfare efforts proved, but few would deny the emergence of sharply felt divisions within the white population. Some of these conflicts originated in political differences—opposing sentiments of Unionism and pro-southernism. Yet in many cases economic and class resentments intensified the oppositions. As we shall see, the passage of a measure exempting supervisors of twenty or more slaves from conscription provoked especially vocal resentment about the wartime meaning of privilege within southern society. In some regions, most notably border areas like Missouri and Kentucky, tensions escalated to the point that many civilians themselves became victims of the violence of Civil War. Even in North Carolina, differences that tended most often to express themselves in the realm of Confederate politics erupted into violence on numerous occasions. In January 1863, for example soldiers murdered thirteen suspected

FREDERICKSBURG, VA:
NURSES AND OFFICERS OF THE U.S. SANITARY COMMISSION.
❈

Unionists, including boys thirteen and fourteen years old. Novelist Charles Frazier has made the exploits of the bands of raiders seeking out deserters widely known through his best seller, *Cold Mountain*. Military service was a frequent focus of such tensions and hostilities as the exemption of slave managers from conscription laws introduced a wedge between the approximately 25% of the white population that owned slaves and the 75% that did not. Women, too, became embroiled in the controversy—most notably in bread riots that erupted in Richmond and locations across the Confederacy in 1863 and later. An eloquent but barely educated North Carolina woman named Nancy Mangum wrote feelingly to Governor Zebulon Vance in 1863: "I have threatened for some time to write you a letter—a crowd of we poor women went to Greensborough yesterday for some-thing to eat as we had not a mouthful meat nor bread—what did they do but put us in jail—we women will write for our husbands to come home and help us." Historian Paul Escott has described these divisions in North Carolina as so extensive as to have constituted an "internal war." Ongoing work by Daniel Sutherland will furnish us with a portrait of far more extensive guerrilla action against civilians across the South than has heretofore been acknowledged. Civilian deaths in the wartime

South have almost certainly been underestimated. Under such circumstances, the distinction between home front and battlefront begins to blur; the violence of war was far from the exclusive province of the military.

Historians have vigorously debated the impact of this dissent and division upon Confederate survival and military effectiveness—most specifically on desertion rates and economic productivity. But these discussions have for the most part overlooked a critical characteristic of the southern home front: if four out of five white men of military age were absent in the army, the Confederate home front was overwhelmingly a world of white women and slaves. How might the recognition of this fact change our understanding both of the home front experience and of its relationship to war's outcome? Louisa Walton reported that her South Carolina community had by 1862 been "thinned out of men." Margaret Junkin Preston of Lexington, Virginia described "a world of femininity with a thin line of boys and octogenarians." In Shelby County, Alabama, 1600 of 1800 white males were in the army. What was the significance of such demographic shifts?

The burgeoning literature on southern women and the war has introduced new perspectives into the consideration of the southern home front. While scholars have explored the relationship of women's actions to the compelling issue of Confederate defeat, they have not confined their analysis to the issue of women's impact on the war. Equally significant has been an investigation of how the war affected women and gender roles more broadly. What were the consequences, to use the words of one Confederate female, of women's "trying to do a man's business" in response to war's exigencies? As women took up men's responsibilities, managing farms and plantations, working for remuneration for the first time, providing their own support, their understandings of themselves were profoundly challenged. In a study of Augusta, Georgia, LeeAnn Whites re-frames the Civil War as a "crisis in gender," noting that definitions of manhood and womanhood were profoundly destabilized by the conflict. Whites believes the power of southern masculinity to have been ultimately reinstated in war's aftermath, but she, like a number of other historians, describes a rethinking of gender categories and a new understanding of their mutability among women of the postwar South.

During the war, southern white women of the poorer classes of necessity undertook an unprecedented level of physically demanding agricultural labor. In search of support for their families, many toiled for the Confederate Clothing Bureau, sewing uniforms for a paltry wage, thirty cents for an entire shirt, for example. Arsenal workers in Augusta made cartridges for a dollar a day. In Richmond, forty female ordnance workers were killed in an 1863 explosion; fifteen died in similar circumstances in Jackson, Mississippi. By the last years of the war, munitions workers in Richmond had become so dissatisfied and desperate they struck for higher wages. Ladies of the privileged ranks confronted new work responsibilities as well. Some few found themselves sometimes forced into the fields; more often, they assumed new duties managing slaves, or entering the workforce as teachers, government employees or hospital matrons, areas of southern life all but closed to women in the prewar years. In the fall of 1862, the Confederate Congress authorized women to serve officially in Confederate hospitals because wards managed by females demonstrated far lower mortality rates. Yet only a few respectable middle or upper class women worked as matrons or nurses. Caring for mens' bodies seemed demeaning and indelicate; most of the more privileged females supervised the wards or visited the sick while slaves or poorer white women bandaged, bathed and fed the soldiers. Many white women were compelled by the war to seek remunerative work for the first time. Teaching seemed an obvious prospect because of women's traditional nurturing roles. Northern women had flocked to classrooms in the prewar years, but no similar development had taken place in the South. In North Carolina in 1860, for example, only 7% of teachers were women. By the end of the war, there were as many females as males in the classroom. For the most part, however, white southern women of the middle and upper classes regarded their new roles as necessity, not opportunity; no rhetoric of liberation or empowerment accompanied these shifts. George Rable has described white women's experience as "change without change." In my own work, I have portrayed white southern women after Appomattox simultaneously frightened about continuing dependence on defeated and seemingly unreliable white men, yet at the same time eager to retreat from wartime's burdens of independence.

Race played a critical role in resolving these contradictions and influencing white women to embrace a reinstatement of patriarchy. The advantages of whiteness and the protections of femininity remained too precious to abandon. War's most trying burden for white women of the slaveholding classes had proved to be its transfer of responsibility for managing slaves onto their shoulders. When white men departed for war, Confederate women assumed the duty of controlling the region's four million slaves. Despite an ideology that celebrated slaves' loyalty and docility, white women expressed profound anxieties about the possibility of slave insurrection and violence. "I fear the blacks more than I do the Yankees," a Mississippi woman declared. Virginian Ellen Moore complained that in her husband's absence her slaves "all think that I am a kind of usurper and have no authority over them." Indeed, a federal officer reported that slaves who fled to Union lines shared her sentiments: "They said there was nobody on the plantations but women and children and they were not afraid of them." Living with slavery in wartime, one Virginia woman observed, was "living with enemies in our own households."

Many white women found the daily acts of coercion and domination slavery required at odds with their understandings of themselves as females. Slaves clearly perceived this crisis of authority and confronted women's doubts, uncertainties and inexperience as managers with enhanced assertiveness and resistance. The difficulties of controlling slaves in the changed wartime environment led many white women to regard the institution as more trouble than benefit. As Sarah Kennedy of Tennessee declared in 1863, she "would rather do all the work rather than be worried with a house full of servants that do what, how and when they please." Their experiences as slave managers seriously eroded their support for the purposes of the war.

The ineffectiveness of many white women in what they and their slaves saw as the essentially contradictory role of female masters played an important part in the disintegration of the peculiar institution in the Confederate South. A vigorous recent historical debate has focused on the question of how freedom came. Expressed most starkly, the question is whether Lincoln freed the slaves by government action or whether the slaves freed themselves through thousands of acts of flight, rebellion and resistance that ultimately destroyed the system from within. What seems to me most striking about this debate is not so much the controversy, but the broad agreement on both sides about the powerful impact of slaves' agency in the Civil War South. No one in this debate embraces a notion of slave loyalty and docility; all agree that the institution of slavery was in considerable upheaval behind Confederate lines. This consensus is critical to our conception of the Confederate home front, for it offers an image of profound disruption, dissension and conflict at the heart of the wartime social order. The Civil War took place not just on the battlefield, not just on the home front between different classes of whites, but even within slave owning households—between women and their servants, between owners and their supposed property within the context of everyday life. From the slaves who smothered their mistress, to those who put salt in the coffee or refused to work on Saturdays or after sundown, to those who fled to freedom or to Union military service, African Americans in the wartime South embraced means of claiming new roles for themselves and of undermining the Confederate social order. Slaves did not rise in open revolt, as had been the case in Saint-Domingue during the French Revolution. "Whenever possible," Vincent Harding has written, they "avoided the deadly prospects of massive, sustained confrontation for their ultimate objective was freedom, not martyrdom." They were, in the words of South Carolina Civil War diarist Mary Chesnut, "biding their time," waiting for means and opportunity for liberation. But we should not underestimate the violence that their efforts to claim freedom produced. Although we can offer numbers that at least approximately quantify the extent of the war's military casualties—620,000—we will never be able to describe civilian death rates with even this precision. But I am constantly struck as I read manuscript materials from the Confederacy by the incidences of violence arising from the conflict over slavery within the South—on its farms and plantations. Some masters shot slaves to keep them from joining the Union army or, in fits of rage, beat female slaves to death after their husbands had fled. For their part, slaves on at least one plantation banded together to give a cruel master a whipping like the ones they had so long endured. The fear and actuality of racial violence were a central component of life on the Confederate home front—not in the form of organized insurrection, but in innumerable day-to-day atrocities arising from the determination of blacks to be free and of whites to prevent them from achieving their goal. These conflicts remind us as well that in an important sense there existed separate black and white home fronts in the South. While one race faced profound challenge to its power, its assumptions, its very existence, the other could regard war's disruptions as opportunity.

Work on the northern home front has been more diffuse and less abundant than this recent outpouring of writing about the Confederacy. In considerable measure, this is because war was less of a presence in northern society: a smaller proportion of men left home to fight; a smaller proportion of the north's resources were expended on the war; enemy troops did not for the most part march across northern soil. As a result, it is more difficult to identify shared wartime experiences or to produce generalizations about war's impact at home.

One outcome of this dilemma is that some of the best recent work on northern wartime society has taken the form of community studies, explorations where a town or city becomes the organizing framework for looking at war. There have also been community studies of southern locales—Daniel Sutherland's on Culpeper County, Virginia; Wayne Durrill on Washington County, North Carolina, for example—but the community study offers a particularly valuable analytic perspective on northern society, for it enables the historian to explore dimensions of life that continued apart from war's influence as well as the impact of the conflict itself. Yet these studies have so far not offered a consistent portrait of what war meant in the North, despite the rich detail they offer about day-to-day lives. Matthew Gallman, for example, argues for little significant change as a result of the war in Philadelphia; Theodore Karamanski sees Chicago "forever transformed." A huge expansion in the meat packing industry—to supply army needs—revolutionized Chicago's labor market and political structures, as well as the lives of city residents for decades to come. Phillip Paludan has argued that the North's war experience must be conceptualized in terms of communities because "northerners had learned the meaning of self-government in these small places" and it was thus for the survival of these cherished communities—and for that of America as democracy's "last best hope on earth"—that northerners fought.

Unlike most southerners, many northerners were not called upon to confront the economic hardships that characterized the Confederate South. Agriculture, which employed 3,500,000 of the North's 5,000,000 workers in 1860, flourished during the conflict. As Paludan notes, "economically the war brought most farmers the best years of their lives." The departure of men for the army raised wages of agricultural laborers, encouraged more rapid mechanization, such as further spread of the reaper, and increased the responsibilities of northern, like southern, women for the day to day labor of farming. The demands for foodstuffs from the army and from the North's growing urban population generated significant increases in market involvement, and rural families found themselves by war's end much more tied to the commercial economy. The Homestead Act of 1862 opened millions of acres of new farmland to upwardly and westwardly mobile settlers, seemingly affirming the Union's commitment to the independent yeoman and to the ideals of free labor.

The experience of the North's industrial laborers was more bleak. Industrial workers served in the army at a high rate, and although their families received military bounties and wages from absent men, many women and children faced hardships in the context of the war's inflationary economy. Most wartime workers experienced an actual decline in their standard of living, a decrease that was even sharper for women laborers than for men, and more dramatic for unskilled than skilled laborers. Tens of thousands of children were drawn into the workforce as well to help replace manpower lost to the war. Although deprivation was neither as widespread nor as intense as in the Confederate South, many on the northern home front, especially in urban areas, also suffered as a result of the war. By 1865, for example, the city of Philadelphia had meted out $2.6 million in an effort to provide support for needy soldiers' families.

Such pressures contributed to growing labor activism, thousands of strikes and many new unions. But the opportunity to stigmatize resisting workers with charges of disloyalty and hindrance of the war effort enhanced the power of owners who were already benefitting from the consolidation of business and wealth encouraged by the war. Much of the intensification of class conflict that resulted from these transformations would not make its appearance until the labor battles of the 1870s and after, but the North did not escape the wartime fissures that rent southern society. Conscription became a focus of much of this conflict, for the slogan "a rich man's war and a poor man's fight" took on special resonance in the context of the economic shifts I have described. The most dramatic manifestations of these divisions were, of course, the New York City draft riots of July 1863. Beginning with an attack on draft offices and upon the wealthy who could escape conscription by paying a commutation fee, the rioters soon redirected their hostility toward black New York, murdering African Americans and burning an orphanage to the ground. As Phillip Paludan has written, "These were the people at the bottom of New York City's society, angered by their suffering, fearful of further inroads on their lives, resentful of both those above them, whose money protected them, and those below them, who seemed potential beneficiaries of the war now that emancipation was a goal. Suffering, envy, hatred, all served to spark the uprising." In the North, as in the South, war brought to the surface deep-seated hostilities of both race and class.

Although the northern home front did not display the same sort of demographic shift toward female predominance as did the South, northern women's lives were also profoundly changed by the war. In a two-volume *History of Woman Suffrage*, published in 1882, Elizabeth Cady Stanton, Susan B. Anthony, and Matilda Gage hailed the war as transformative. "The social and political condition of women was largely changed by our Civil War," they wrote. "In large measure," they explained, it was because war "created a revolution in woman herself."

One of the areas of women's participation that has gained most attention in this regard was nursing. In the South, most women who entered hospital work during the war were erstwhile volunteers or visitors, rather than long-term salaried hospital workers, and their labors were more likely to prove a temporary extension of the domain of nurturant domesticity than a lasting transgression of conventional gender boundaries. Northern nurses, by contrast, were more likely to use their wartime experiences as a foundation for a new sense of self and vocation. In the North, the war provided a catalyst for women's advancement into both professional nursing and medicine. The lives of Clara Barton and Dorothea Dix exemplify this northern pattern, one which leads historian Elizabeth Leonard to conclude that northern nurses "trespassed en masse into the 'public sphere,'" and became "wielders of a new kind of institutional power previously hoarded by men."

Women's wartime activism in the North grew directly out of prewar traditions of reform and focused on a variety of goals: abolition, first and foremost; Lincoln's reelection, female suffrage, and philanthropic efforts for soldiers and their families. As with studies of white southern women, however, the question remains of how empowering and transformative these undertakings proved. Matthew Gallman's study of Philadelphia shows women engaged in a broadening array of benevolent efforts, but he does not see a concomitant rise in their authority. In larger organizations, women volunteers tended to labor under male directors. Lori Ginzberg's study of northern wartime benevolence identifies gender conflicts between male and female philanthropists. She concludes that an older female style of benevolence was replaced by a masculine gospel of charitable efficiency that eclipsed not just female values but women themselves.

Despite Stanton, Anthony and Gage's triumphant assessment, the legacy of war for northern women seems ultimately to have been mixed. The attention of these nineteenth-century writers was, we should note, in any case directly—almost exclusively—to the meaning of the war in the lives of middle-class women like themselves, and so they took little account of working women pressured by war's economic circumstances. Women regarded work as a burden rather than an opportunity and swelled the ranks of the North's manufacturing labor force during the conflict. But even for the ranks of more privileged women who were their subjects, Stanton, Anthony and Gage may have been overly optimistic. As Elizabeth Leonard recently concluded, the northern "gender system in the end demonstrated remarkable rigidity at its core." Yet its rigidity, its resistance to change, was not as great as in the South; wartime experiences of middle-class northern women encouraged many to imagine the possibility of different lives, as the postwar entry of women into medicine attests. Stanton and Anthony may in fact have derived their triumphalism from their own first-hand knowledge of the impact of war's democratic ferment upon the movement for woman suffrage. Although they would be bitterly disappointed when the fifteenth Amendment enfranchised black men but not white women, Stanton and Anthony believed that the foundation for women's ultimate success in achieving the vote was assured by the victory of the ideologies of citizenship and human rights for which the North fought.

The centrality of gender to war's meaning for the North has assumed an additional dimension in recent work on masculinity, on the way soldiers defined themselves and their purposes in relationship to a "female domestic sphere." The home was critical, Reid Mitchell has argued, to the soldier's motivation to fight and to his understanding of himself; just before the battle he thought not of politics or God or death, Mitchell believes, but mother. Here we have another rendering of a theme we have seen throughout our considerations of home front North and South: the profound and abiding connections between home and battlefront, the way the two can blur in the context of Civil War experience. This was certainly true for many civilians, particularly southerners, whose homes and farms became battlefields—like Wilmer McLean who hosted the First Battle of Manassas, the first major conflict of the war, on his northern Virginia farm in 1861, then moved South to Appomattox to entertain Grant and Lee in his parlor four years later. Home and battlefront seem to merge as well in the incidences of serious conflict and violence amongst civilians distant from war's front lines. In draft riots in the North, food riots in the South, in the erupting tensions of a disintegrating slave system, hostilities and violent confrontation moved beyond the battlefield both to enlist and victimize civilians. And battle and home front joined as well in the close links of influence and motivation that tied them together. Men enlisted to protect women or deserted for the same end. Soldiers fought for homes and communities which in turn became an overarching rationale for commitment and sacrifice.

Yet our understanding of what we call the "home front" remains partial and incomplete. Dozens of topics that would enhance our understanding of the war have been overlooked entirely or are only beginning to be explored. Let me speak of two such neglected dimensions of life central to nineteenth-century Americans—North and South—and central to their experience of Civil War. The first is religion. Both the Union and the Confederacy believed that God was on its side. Religion was at the heart of the soldiers' reasons for fighting and their consolations for dying; it was a foundation of strength for civilians sacrificing their loved ones to the cause; it was a motivation for slaves struggling for the Day of Jubilee. The language of the war was cast in religious metaphor, as both sides worried about God's chastening hand. Yet as three prominent scholars recently observed, "the religious history of the war has yet to be written." A recent collection of essays about religion and the Civil War is designed as an invitation to further research and inquiry, for this is a topic both military and home front historians need to understand far better. It is also another example of a force linking the civilian with the military experience and reaching across any division between home and battlefront.

The second area I want just to mention is the focus of my own current research: the subject of death in the Civil War. With such an enormous rate of death in the army, nearly all Americans were touched by the war's impact. Indeed, death may have been the most powerful Civil War reality for many Americans. Obviously it was so for those who actually died, but for survivors as well, the deaths of loved ones, comrades, neighbors may have proved the most powerfully felt of all the Civil War's experiences. I think we need to know far more about the meaning of this slaughter for the generation that lived through it. And as I have already suggested, it seems to me highly probable that we have seriously underestimated the number of civilian deaths that resulted from the war. Contagious diseases brought to cities and towns by encamped troops killed more than just soldiers; the disruptions of slavery brought the kinds of violence and retribution I have already described; the irregular warfare of the conflict may well have been, as Daniel Sutherland is beginning to show, far more extensive than we have heretofore imagined.

The Civil War home front offers rich opportunities for historical research and exploration which scholars are investigating in growing numbers and with increasing sophistication. The studies of the decade to come are likely to enhance our understanding at least as greatly as those of the decade just past. And as we understand more about the home front, we will be compelled to reconfigure our assumptions about the battlefront as well, for, as I have tried to suggest here, the division between the two in a conflict like the American Civil War is often arbitrary. Both battle and home front played a significant role in the outcome of the war and in the experience of every one of war's participants.

Suggestions for further reading:

Ash, Stephen. *When the Yankees Came: Conflict and Chaos in the Occupied South, 1861-1865.* Chapel Hill: University of North Carolina Press, 1995.

Attie, Jeanie. *Patriotic Toil: Northern Women and the American Civil War.* Ithaca: Cornell University Press, 1998.

Blair, William. *Virginia's Private War: Feeding Body and Soul in the Confederacy, 1861-1865.* New York: Oxford University Press, 1998.

Berlin, Ira and Leslie Rowland, eds., *Families and Freedom: A Documentary History of African American Kinship in the Civil War Era.* New York: New Press, 1997.

Berlin, Ira. et al., *Free At Last: A Documentary History of Slavery, Freedom and the Civil War.* New York: New Press, 1992.

Bernstein, Iver. *The New York City Draft Riots.* New York: Oxford University Press, 1990.

Campbell, Edward D.C. and Kym Rice. *A Woman's War: Southern Women, Civil War, and the Confederate Legacy.* Charlottesville: University Press of Virginia, 1996.

Clinton, Catherine and Nina Silber, eds., *Divided Houses: Gender and the Civil War.* New York: Oxford University Press, 1992.

Durrill, Wayne K. *War of Another Kind: A Southern Community in the Great Rebellion.* New York: Oxford, 1990.

Faust, Drew Gilpin. *Mothers of Invention: Women of the Slaveholding South in the American Civil War.* Chapel Hill: University of North Carolina Press, 1996.

Fellman, Michael. *Inside War: The Guerrilla Conflict in Missouri During the American Civil War.* New York: Oxford University Press, 1989.

Gallman, J. Matthew. *Mastering Wartime: A Social History of Philadelphia During the Civil War.* New York: Cambridge University Press, 1990.

_____. *The North Fights the Civil War: The Home Front.* Chicago: Ivan Dee, 1994.

Ginzberg, Lori D. *Women and the Work of Benevolence: Morality, Politics and Class in the Nineteenth Century. United States.* New Haven: Yale University Press, 1990.

Karamanski, Theodore. *Rally Round the Flag: Chicago and the Civil War.* Chicago: Nelson-Hall, 1993.

Leonard, Elizabeth. *Yankee Women: Gender Battles in the Civil War.* New York: Norton, 1994.

Marten, James. *The Children's Civil War.* Chapel Hill: University of North Carolina Press, 1998.

Miller, Randall M., Harry S. Stout and Charles Reagan Wilson, eds., *Religion and the American Civil War.* New York: Oxford University Press, 1998.

Mitchell, Reid. *The Vacant Chair: The Northern Soldier Leaves Home.* New York: Oxford University Press,

1993.

Paludan, Phillip Shaw. *A People's Contest: The Union and Civil War*. New York: Harper and Row, 1988.

Rable, George. *Civil Wars: Women and the Crisis of Southern Nationalism*. Urbana: University of Illinois Press, 1989.

Sutherland, Daniel E., ed., *Guerrillas, Unionists and Violence on the Confederate Home Front*. Fayetteville: University of Arkansas Press, 1999.

Sutherland, Daniel E. *Seasons of War: The Ordeal of a Confederate Community, 1861-1865*. New York: Free Press, 1995.

Whites, LeeAnn. *The Civil War as a Crisis in Gender: Augusta, Georgia, 1860-1890*. Athens: University of Georgia Press, 1995.

THE CIVIL WAR AND A NEW BIRTH OF AMERICAN FREEDOM

by Eric Foner

What is freedom? How do Americans view this ideal? And, how did the Civil War shape the concept of and American's view of freedom? The word freedom has been used so frequently and in so many contexts it has become a cliché. Today, anti-government militia groups passionately claim ownership of the concept of freedom. Conversely, American liberals view empowerment of all people through civil rights and economic opportunity as the proper definition of freedom. Clearly, then, there is no consistent, universal meaning for the term freedom. But, as Professor Foner argues, the American Civil War redefined the meaning of freedom and expanded the entitlement of its blessings in profound ways. For, as Abraham Lincoln said at Gettysburg, the Civil War ushered in a new birth of freedom.

Introduced by John Latschar
Gettysburg National Military Park

It is a great pleasure to take part in this symposium. I have the utmost regard for the National Park Service. The difficulty its directors and interpreters face in conveying history at these sites makes what we do in the classroom look awfully easy. But regardless of the criticisms and grounds for improvement, we academic historians really do appreciate the way you are bringing history to millions of Americans every year. I am going to talk about what Dwight Pitcaithley called the "so what" aspect of the Civil War—some of the war's consequences. More precisely, I am going to talk about what the war means for us today for understanding who we are as a people, as a nation. The subject today is drawn from the Gettysburg address, which, of course, was given at what is now the Gettysburg National Military Park.

The Civil War was "a new birth of freedom" for the United States. Now, I do not need to persuade you that there is no idea more central to our conception of ourselves as Americans than freedom. This is the central word in our political vocabulary, and between freedom and its twin word—liberty—you can find these concepts in just about every key document of American history. The Declaration of Independence lists liberty as one of the inalienable rights of man. The Constitution announces that its purpose is to secure the blessings of liberty. The Civil War brought about "a new birth of freedom," as Lincoln said. The United States fought World War II for the Four Freedoms, according to President Franklin D. Roosevelt. Our love of liberty has been represented by liberty poles, liberty caps, and statues of liberty. It has been acted out by burning stamps and burning draft cards, by running away from slavery and by demonstrating for the right to vote. As Ralph Bunch wrote in 1940, "every man in the street, white, black, red, or yellow knows that this is the land of the free."

But, despite the centrality of freedom in our history, this concept is not fixed, not predetermined, but has changed many times in American history, and is constantly the subject of controversy and even very bitter battles. What is freedom? Who has the right to determine what freedom is? Who has the right to determine who is entitled to freedom? Does freedom encompass everybody who happens to be within the boundaries of the United States, or are some people entitled to more freedom than others? These debates have continued throughout our history and will continue into the next century. I have no doubt of that.

Today, if you have some spare time, use your trusty computer and search the Internet looking for freedom. You will find some very strange things. You will find that the term freedom mostly is associated with anti-government libertarians, people who believe in free market economics and especially in the right to bear arms. Patriotic organizations, militia organizations, these are the groups today who most insistently use the word freedom. The website of the extremist group, the Militia of Montana, is emblazoned with this expression: "It's Your Choice: Freedom Or Slavery." They are not talking about the slavery we have discussed in this symposium. Even so mainstream a corporation as Sony Pictures has a website promoting a forthcoming movie *The Patriot*, set in the American Revolution and starring Mel Gibson. On this website, Sony has a little bulletin board with the title "Discuss Freedom," where individuals can give their views. Here, you will find comments that say gun ownership should take precedence over all other freedoms, it is our most precious freedom. There is also a modern American declaration of liberty modeled on the Declaration of Independence of 1776 with various complaints against the federal government including the income tax, welfare, economic regulation and membership in the United Nations. This is what freedom seems to mean today. But it hasn't always had that meaning. The Civil War, among many other things, was a crisis concerning the meaning of freedom in this country and it produced a redefinition of freedom in American history. The "new birth of freedom" that Lincoln spoke about was also a fundamental change in what American freedom was and who was entitled to it.

Both sides in the Civil War fought in the name of freedom. Many who took up arms in the cause of southern independence wrote about it as a struggle for liberty. The white South had inherited from the antebellum period an understanding of freedom that centered on local self-government, opportunities for economic independence and security of property including property in slaves. Indeed, many southern whites believed that slavery was the foundation of liberty. "I am engaged in the glorious cause of liberty and justice," wrote an Alabama soldier in 1862, with no more sense of irony than Thomas Jefferson had when he wrote of the "inalienable right" to liberty while he owned over a hundred slaves. To own slaves was a very good way of ensuring one's economic independence, which was one of the foundations of liberty in the nineteenth century.

Union soldiers, of course, also spoke about what one Pennsylvania recruit called the "magic word freedom." They saw the war as an effort to preserve the United States as what Lincoln called "the last, best hope of earth;" or "the beacon of liberty and freedom," as one soldier wrote, "to the human race." But as the war progressed, these abstract definitions of America as the symbol of liberty began to give way to a more concrete meaning of freedom tied to the emancipation of the slaves. Millions of northerners who had not been abolitionists when the war began became convinced that securing the Union as the embodiment of liberty required the destruction of slavery. This was Lincoln's meaning when he spoke about "the new birth of freedom," or when he told Congress in December 1862 on the eve of the Emancipation Proclamation, "in giving freedom to the slave we ensure freedom to the free, honorable alike in what we give and what we preserve." Emancipation, as Lincoln came to believe, was essential to maintaining the freedom of white America and the United States itself as an emblem of liberty to the entire world. Lincoln also commented, during the Civil War, on how variable and contested this notion of freedom was. "We all declare for liberty" he observed in 1864, "but in using the same word, we do not mean the same thing. To the North," he went on, freedom meant "for every man to enjoy the product of his labor, to work and enjoy the fruits of his labor. To southern whites, it meant mastership, the power," as he said, "to do as they please with other men and the product of other men's labor." To Lincoln, ultimately, slavery was a form of theft, stealing the products of labor of one person and appropriating it by another. The Union's triumph consolidated this northern vision of freedom as control over your own person and over your power to labor as the national norm. But in the process, the meaning of freedom and the definition of those who were entitled to enjoy liberty were very radically transformed.

Throughout American history, wars have helped to change the conception of American society. The War for Independence led to the abolition of slavery in the northern states. Women won the right to vote after World War I, eighteen-year-olds gained this privilege during the War in Vietnam. The Union's victory in 1865 also led to searching discussions over this question of American nationality. "Who is an American?" Wendell Phillips, the great abolitionist commented in 1866, "it is a singular fact that unlike all other nations, this nation has yet a question as to what constitutes a citizen." From the Civil War emerged a new principle, that of a national citizenship whose members enjoyed the equal protection of the laws regardless of race. It redefined the boundary of the American nation—not the physical boundary, although it did that—but the nation's imagined boundary. Early in 1865, the Supreme Court, which eight years earlier in the Dred Scott decision had declared that no black person could be a citizen, admitted the first African American lawyer, John Rock of Boston, to practice law before it.

"There could no longer be even a shadow of a doubt," wrote Francis Lieber, a writer on political affairs at that time, that blacks were citizens entitled to protection by the federal government. Not only was there a new logic of liberty, but the service of 200,000 black men in the Union army and navy put the question of black citizenship on the nation's post-war agenda. "The inevitable consequence of black military service," as one Senator remarked, was that "the black man is henceforth to assume a new status among us."

That was in 1864. In that same year, Lincoln wrote a private letter to the Governor Michael Hahn of Louisiana, suggesting that some black Americans ought to have the right to vote. What is interesting here is that Lincoln singled out those who were deserving. New Orleans had a rather important population of well-educated, propertied free African Americans who had been petitioning for the suffrage. Lincoln said to Governor Hahn that these educated free Negroes should have the right to vote. But he added as well those who had fought in the Union army, which was a much larger and a very different group. Those who fought in the army were not educated, did not own property; they were, for the most part, former slaves quite unlike the free Negroes in New Orleans. But, Lincoln was tremendously impressed by the contribution that black soldiers made in the last two years of the war to help achieve Union victory.

Racism was hardly eradicated from American life by the Civil War. But by 1865, declared George William Curtis, the editor of *Harpers Weekly* magazine, the war had transformed "a government for white men into a government for mankind." It erased the racial definition of American citizenship, which had existed from the founding fathers down to the Civil War. And by redrawing this boundary of citizenship, the war tied the progress of liberty directly to the power of the national state. "War," declared the nineteenth-century German historian Heinrich von Treitschke, "turns a people into a nation." The Civil War was begun to preserve the old Union, but it ended up bringing into being a new nation state, a new government with greatly expanded powers.

The war forged national identity into a new national self-consciousness. This was the moral of one of the most popular stories of the war period. We used to read this in school all the time—now it is not so popular—*The Man Without A Country* by Edward Everett Hale, published in 1863. Hale's protagonist, Philip Nolan, in a fit of anger curses the United States, the land of his birth. As punishment, he is condemned to live on a ship never to set foot on American soil or to hear the name of the United States of America uttered. The moral of this story is that to be deprived of national identity is to lose one's sense of self, one's individuality. This new national state was intimately linked to the progress of freedom during the Civil War. The war, as Frederick Douglass said, "merged the cause of the slave and the cause of the country." This was the key to the emancipation of the slaves. The cause of the slave and the cause of the country now became identical.

To be sure, a generation of northern school children had learned to recite Daniel Webster's immortal words spoken on the floor of the Senate in 1830, "Liberty and Union, now and forever, one and inseparable." But Webster was talking about the doctrine of states rights, not the South's peculiar institution of slavery. When Douglass said, thirty years later, that liberty and union had become identical, he was talking about slavery, not political doctrine. Slavery not only was a moral crime but it was an affront to national power. "The master's sovereignty over the slave," said Charles Sumner, the abolitionist senator from Massachusetts, was incompatible with the paramount rights of the national government. Every citizen owed allegiance to the nation. Nobody should owe allegiance to another person the way a slave did. And the destruction of slavery by presidential proclamation, by legislation, and by constitutional amendment was a key act in the nation building process. It announced the appearance of a new kind of national state, one powerful enough to destroy the central institution of southern society.

The drama of emancipation and the triumph of the Union fused together nationalism, morality, and the idea of freedom, a combination underpinned by a religious language as well as a secular one. "As he died to make men holy let us live to make men free," said the "Battle Hymn of the Republic." And those who believed in America's millennial mission to represent freedom in the world interpreted the Civil War as a divine punishment for this divergence from the principle of liberty. Lincoln himself, not a very religious man, came to use this language as the war went on. But emancipation also gave the nation a chance for regeneration, for purging itself of this sin of slavery.

The concrete reality of emancipation made freedom into a political issue, a substantive issue, not just an abstraction or philosophical concept. It raised in the most direct form the question, what are the rights of free Americans? "What is freedom?" Congressman James Garfield asked in 1865. "Is it the bare privilege of not being chained? If this is all, then freedom is a mockery, a cruel delusion." What rights went along with freeing the slaves? Did the freed people have the right to civil equality, to political equality, to ownership of property? If the abolition of slavery reinforced the status of freedom as the key term in our political language, this made the control of the definition of freedom all the more important in political debates. Freedom became a terrain of conflict open to very different and very contradictory interpretations in the wake of the Civil War.

Now, I am going to talk a bit about the period right after the Civil War. If we are going to put the Civil War in context in terms of its causes, we also must think about the consequences of the Civil War and its immediate aftermath, the period of Reconstruction, when the nation tried to deal with the results of Union victory and emancipation. There were many actors—to use a theatrical metaphor—on the stage of history who tried to put forward their own definition of liberty. First among them, were, of course, the former slaves themselves. In bondage, African Americans had forged their own understanding of what freedom would be. Adopting the nation's democratic language as their own, they interpreted it in the light of their own particular traditions and religious beliefs rooted in the biblical story of Exodus, in which a chosen people suffers a long period of bondage eventually to be released through divine intervention. Slaves saw themselves as individuals deprived of rights and as a people lacking self-determination. So, freedom for them meant not getting the government off your back, as it seems to mean today, but escaping the many injustices of slavery, including punishment by the whip, the breaking up of family, denial or access of education, and the sexual exploitation of black women.

Freedom also meant collective empowerment, a share in the rights, entitlements, and opportunities of other Americans. Blacks interpreted the outbreak of the Civil War as God's message that their passage to the promised land of freedom was now at hand. Long before Lincoln declared emancipation a Union war aim, slaves called the war "the freedom war." Acting on this understanding, thousands of slaves in 1861 and '62 fled the plantations when they could and when the Union army came nearby. Their actions placed the future of slavery on the national political agenda. What would you do with these people? Do you return them, do you free them, do you employ them, do you educate them? The Lincoln administration had to start making policies about slavery because of the flight of slaves from plantations.

This was a country that prided itself on democracy. In such a context, the right to vote came to seem essential to freedom. As Frederick Douglass stated in 1865, "slavery is not abolished until the black man has the ballot." To lack the right to vote was to be not fully free in American. In a monarchial government, Douglass continued, there was no special disgrace applied to those denied the right to vote. But, in America, exclusion branded people, as Douglass said, with the "mark of inferiority." As soon as the Civil War ended, and indeed, even before it ended in some areas, blacks in the South came together in meetings, parades, petitions, and in many other ways, demanding the right to vote. Sometimes they organized "freedom ballots," in which they had their own elections, when local white authorities would not let them vote. Anything less than full citizenship, African Americans believed, would betray the promise of emancipation. And of course, black men did eventually get the right to vote during Reconstruction and participated in a remarkable experiment in interracial democracy after the Civil War. Then, after a generation, in the 1890s, one after another, the southern states took the right to vote away from African Americans. And long after they had been stripped of the franchise, blacks would recall the act of voting as an essential element of emancipation, and regard the loss of suffrage as being a step backward toward slavery.

Also crucial to the former slaves' definition of freedom was economic autonomy. When General William T. Sherman met with a group of black ministers in Savannah in January 1865, shortly after his march to the sea he asked them for their definitions of slavery and freedom. The spokesman for these black ministers, Garrison Frazier, offered definitions. "Slavery," said Frazier, "is receiving . . . the work of another man and not by his consent." This was pretty much what Lincoln had said. Freedom, on the other hand, meant "placing us where we can reap the fruit of our own labor." Sherman then asked how they could do that, and they said: "give us land and we can reap the fruit of our labor and then we will be genuinely free." "Only land," said another former slave, "would enable the poor class to enjoy the sweet boon of freedom." What happened after that was that Sherman issued his famous Field Order Number 15, which set aside a band of land on the coast of South Carolina and Georgia for the settlement of black families on forty-acre plots. Sherman also had a lot of mules with his army. Many of them were worn out from dragging things all around Georgia. So, he said these black families were going to get forty acres of land and these broken down mules to help farm the land. This is where the term "forty acres and a mule" comes from. It reverberated throughout the South in the early days of Reconstruction and is about the only thing most students know about Reconstruction today—possibly because it is the name of Spike Lee's film company.

To African Americans, freedom meant many of the same things it meant to white Americans—economic autonomy, family stability, the right to vote, the fruits of your labor, and so forth. But taken together the attitudes of the former slaves had a rather different focus from that of whites. To most white Americans freedom was a birth right to be defended. To African Americans, it was something to struggle toward an open-ended process and millennial transformation of every aspect of their lives. Many whites used the term "slavery" to define themselves in the nineteenth century. The labor movement talked about wage slavery, the women's movement talked about the slavery of sex. Slavery was a powerful metaphor for lack of rights. But, of course, to blacks it was not a metaphor. Slavery

"THE FIRST VOTE."—DRAWN BY A. R. WAUD.—[SEE NEXT PAGE.]

ALFRED R. WAUD'S "THE FIRST VOTE," OCTOBER 1867.

was a traumatic real experience, which for many, many years afterwards would help to shape their conception of themselves and of their American society.

Of course, African Americans were not the only actors on the stage trying to put forward a definition of freedom. Southern whites—especially the planter class—had their own version of what freedom was. And, in the aftermath of the Civil War, white southerners, aided and abetted by President Andrew Johnson, tried to keep black freedom confined within the narrowest conceivable boundaries. As northern journalist Sidney Andrews wrote late in 1865 traveling around the South: "The whites seem wholly unable to comprehend that freedom for the Negro demands the same thing as freedom for them. They readily enough admit that the government has made him free but they appear to believe that they have the right to exercise the same old control." Most white southerners believed that the plantation system had to be maintained after slavery, which meant that African Americans could not be given the choice as to whether or not they wanted to work on plantations. They had to be coerced into doing so. They would receive some wages or a share of the crop, but they would not have the choice as their white counterparts of other occupations.

Freedom still meant hierarchy in society. It still meant mastery over subordinates, as it had before the Civil War. Freedom for white southerners was still a privilege to be enjoyed by some, not an entitlement of everybody. "A man may be free yet not independent," wrote one planter. In other words, it didn't mean giving blacks land. "A man can be free and not have the right to vote." said another. Freedom had a very narrow definition. One Kentucky newspaper summed all this up by saying, "the former slave is free, but free only to labor." The former slave's role was to work as he or she had under slavery and no other rights came along with emancipation. And indeed, this vision was put into law in the early days of Presidential Reconstruction in 1865–66. The so-called Black Codes, which southern states passed to regulate the transition from freedom, tried to force former slaves to go back to work on the plantations and to sign labor contracts, giving them no political rights whatsoever.

These laws so flagrantly violated the meaning of emancipation that they aroused a great deal of hostility in the North, and catalyzed the momentous conflict between President Andrew Johnson and the Republican Congress. This conflict eventually led to his impeachment, to the overthrow of Presidential Reconstruction, and to the enactment of civil rights laws and constitutional amendments that put the new definition of freedom into the basic laws of our land. Much of the conflict over Reconstruction revolved around the definition of freedom. The Republican majority in Congress operated on the principle that freedom required equality before the law for all Americans. That was the principle of the Civil Rights Act of 1866 and the Fourteenth Amendment. These actions established for the first time in American history a principle we take for granted—which was a new thing in 1866—the principle of birthright citizenship. This is one of the most momentous legacies of the Civil War, the principle that anybody born in the United States is a citizen. This was not the case before the Civil War. The Supreme Court ruled in 1857, in the Dred Scott decision, that no black person could be a citizen, born here or not, free or slave. Citizenship was for white Americans.

Equality before the law was a completely new thing in American history as well. There was not a state in the Union that gave black people legal equality before the Civil War. Even Massachusetts, which came close, still prohibited blacks from joining the state militia, for example. Every state, North and South, had special laws relating to blacks. Certain things were crimes if a black did them, as opposed to a white doing them. Certain punishments were harsher if a black committed the crime than if a white committed the same crime. So this dual principle of birthright citizenship and equality before the law—that the law must apply the same to everybody regardless of race—these were the products of the Civil War.

If anyone wants to know why the Civil War is relevant today, these are some of the reasons. It created our modern conception of what it is to be a citizen of the United States. These laws affected everybody; they did not just expand the definition of freedom for blacks. These principles have reverberated throughout time, and have affected every immigrant who has come into the country. Until the 1940s, Asian immigrants could not become naturalized citizens, yet their American-born children were automatically citizens. So the generational gap among Asian Americans, between the immigrant non-citizen and the children citizen, this harks back to the Fourteenth Amendment and the principle of birthright citizenship.

The Fourteenth Amendment also had another powerful effect on what the American nation became. By inserting into the Constitution the new concept of the empowered national state, it not only established a new definition of freedom, it provided a new mode for enforcing this freedom. Rather than a threat to liberty, the state that emerged out of the Civil War was seen, in the words of Charles Sumner, as "the custodian of freedom." The Fourteenth Amendment made the federal government responsible for overriding state actions that interfered with the rights of citizens. One can understand what this means in very clear terms by examining the Thirteenth, Fourteenth, and Fifteenth amendments to the Constitution—the Civil War Reconstruction Amendments. The Thirteenth abolished slavery, the Fourteenth established equal citizenship, and the Fifteenth granted black men the right to vote.

Compare the language of those amendments to the Bill of Rights, which are seen as the embodiment of our liberties. The Bill of Rights is a series of negations or restrictions on Congress: Congress shall pass no law abridging the freedom of speech, press, and religion. The principle of the Bill of Rights is that a too powerful federal government will trample on our liberties. It is not until the twentieth century that the Supreme Court declared that states must abide by or recognize the liberties in the Bill of Rights. The Thirteenth, Fourteenth, and Fifteenth amendments end with a clause, which says: Congress shall have the power to "enforce" the amendment by "appropriate legislation." Thus, the paradigm changed from "Congress shall pass no law" to "Congress shall have the power." This is a clear example of the shift in federalism toward an empowered national government having the paramount responsibility for protecting the rights of citizens. The Civil War Reconstruction amendments made the Constitution a different document from what it had been.

Today, we hear political debates about going back to the original intent of the framers of the Constitution. That theory ignores the fact that the Constitution has changed fundamentally. Before the Civil War, disenfranchised groups never cited the Constitution to claim their rights; instead; they cited the Declaration of Independence. The Constitution was a document concerned with federal-state relations and the rights of property, not the rights of citizens. After the Civil War, the Constitution became a vehicle through which minorities and others could stake a claim to freedom and seek their rights.

While the Civil War and Reconstruction amendments radically changed the federal government regarding the protection of the rights of minorities, prevailing conventions of gender proved more resistant to change than racial conventions. The Civil War consolidated a movement among activist women to claim their rights as well. "The re-writing of the Constitution," as one feminist leader said, "offered the opportunity to sever the rights of citizens from race and sex, two accidents of the body." "We must bury the black man and the woman in the citizen," said another. The black man temporarily obtained rights. This did not happen for women, as we know. Indeed, the women's movement was bitterly disappointed by the Fourteenth Amendment, which introduced the word "male" into the Constitution for the first time. And, if that were not enough, the Fifteenth Amendment protected suffrage on the basis of race, but left open the possibility of discrimination in suffrage on the basis of gender, which was common in all states at that time. So, the women's movement had a long way to go before achieving its rights.

The expansion of freedom in the Civil War was not total, but it changed the definition of who was entitled to American liberty. African American males gained, but then lost the right to vote. The desire of the former slaves for land met with disappointment as well. Efforts in Congress to give the former slaves land, led by Thaddeus Stevens—the Congressman from Pennsylvania—did not receive majority support. By the 1870s, reconciliation and reunion were more important than rights and freedom. Part of the cost of reunion was forgetting why the Civil War had been fought, and pushing to the side the rights that African Americans had won in its aftermath.

I will conclude by saying that in retrospect the era of the Civil War and Reconstruction emerges as a decisive moment in the ongoing and forever unfinished story of freedom in America. It is a story like so many other parts of our history that is both uplifting and sobering. It is uplifting to see four million people move from slavery to freedom, and to see the great struggles which took place to give them their rights as citizens—the great experiment of Reconstruction and the advent of a genuine interracial democracy in the South in that period. It is sobering because, as Thomas Wentworth Higginson, a commander of black soldiers in the Civil War later wrote: "revolutions may go backward." The story of freedom in this country is not a linear story of progress. It is not a story of a predetermined narrative leading to a fixed end of greater liberty. The revolution of the Civil War did go backwards. It would be left to future generations, including our own, to try to give full meaning to the destruction of slavery in 1865.

Questions and Answers:

Question: Isn't it true that greed was the underlying cause of the Civil War and the protection of the institution of slavery?

Answer: As an American I never underestimate the power of greed as a motivating force of human behavior, and certainly slavery originated as a form of making profit. That is why slaves were brought here in the first place to labor for the benefit of others—tobacco planters, cotton planters, and so forth. The Civil War made some people very rich but made some people rather poor, not in the South so much, but certainly in the North. Some people benefited enormously from the Civil War. That said, trying to reduce the question of slavery to a matter of greed, ignores the complex ramifications of this institution. Slavery was a system of labor, a system of economic production, a system of race relations, a system of political power, and a system of morality. All of those elements were involved in the slavery issue and in the Civil War, so it is about money, it is about religion, it is about morality, it is about politics, and it is about ideology. That is what makes the teaching of history complicated and interesting—to try to integrate all these factors into a coherent story of this dramatic period.

Question: To really understand the war, do we not, in a sense, put ourselves back into the minds of southerners in 1860 and what slavery meant to them, trying to put aside our modern views about the evils of slavery, which may make it impossible to really understand what their thoughts were?

Answer: Yes, the answer is we do have to try to go back and put ourselves in the minds of actors of the time. But, by doing that, historians produce many, many interpretations of the Civil War. There is an interpretation that the Civil War was a big mistake; it was, as one book says, a crisis of fear and paranoia. Personally, I believe that any war has its share of paranoia and fear, but I think the wiser approach is to ask why people at the time felt that slavery was such an important institution to them that they were willing to go to war to defend it or the society built upon it. As we know, most southern soldiers were not slave owners, but they had invested in defending their "way of life," which was based on slavery. Even a non-slave owner was defending a society whose fundamental organizing principle revolved around slavery. Most of them would not say "I am fighting for slavery," but they certainly would say "I am opposed to the abolition of slavery because that would destroy southern society as I know it."

One thing that one has to remember is that slavery has existed for most of human history—a sad commentary—and in fact, slavery exists today. There are slaves being bought and sold as we speak in the Sudan and in some other places. The great empires of Greece and Rome were built on slavery.

It is a recent thing in human history, the notion that every human being is entitled to liberty. Slave owners felt that they were, in a sense, the normal people, in relation to world history, and that the people in the North and in Great Britain were the aberrations. This free labor system, this notion of individual equality was a deviation in terms of how the world had existed. That is a frame of mind which is impossible for us to replicate completely, knowing what we know and feeling how we feel. So, to understand both sides of the Civil War, we have to try to get ourselves into the frame of mind of the people then, not the frame of mind of the year 2000. Concerning the issue of slavery, that is not an easy task.

Question: Did Congress abolish slavery in the District of Columbia and compensate the owners?

Answer: Congress abolished slavery in the District of Columbia on April 16, 1862. The act provided for compensation to the owners for up to $300 for each slave. The District of Columbia was under the jurisdiction of Congress; therefore, Congress could do whatever it wanted there, which it could not do with the states. Lincoln proposed compensated emancipation a number of times in 1862. He called on the congressional delegation from Delaware, and offered to pay for the emancipation of slaves in that state. He argued that this was a way of settling the Civil War, and that it would be much cheaper than the cost of the war. But the leaders in Delaware said no—"we do not want your money, but we want our slaves." This was not just a question of money. Some slaveholders in the loyal border states did receive compensation. However, the vast majority of slaves were freed without compensation to the owners, and indeed the Fourteenth Amendment prohibited any compensation for emancipated slaves after that point.

The issue of compensation is relevant today, because of the question of reparations for slavery. Should the descendants of slaves receive reparations, as, for example, today billions of dollars are being appropriated to compensate slave laborers in Nazi Germany? Without commenting on that specific issue, let me say that during the Civil War the issue of compensation related to compensating the masters not the slaves. There were some slaves who said they deserved land as a form of compensation, but the issue in the Civil War was a question of whether or not owners should be compensated for the loss of their property rights in slaves.

Question: Should we place slavery in the context of white supremacy or racism, which was a set of beliefs shared in both North and South? And, under that assumption, should not white majorities have a right to govern themselves and establish whatever form of white supremacy they want?

Answer: I do not disagree at all that racism or white supremacy was a very deeply rooted belief system throughout the country in the nineteenth century, and, indeed, before and after. But I think the danger of simply saying that is to view racism as a constant—it is always there and it never changes. Racism, like anything else, has a history. Its forms change, its strength changes, as does its salience in people's lives. People have many different sets of beliefs at the same time and many kinds of identities. We have seen instances in which white people who might be called racist have gone on strike with black people because they share an economic issue, which may override their racism at that moment. We have seen it work the other way too. We have seen poor white people during the Populist Era in the late 1800s side with planters even though their economic interests were with black farmers.

All of this makes the Civil War and Reconstruction period that much more remarkable. Here was a time when a majority of white northerners actually were willing for numerous reasons—some crass, some noble—to put aside racism and actually do things that seem inconceivable. In 1860, it was absolutely unimaginable that a majority of people in the North would favor a Constitutional amendment giving blacks the right to vote or to take major steps to end discrimination. The Civil War itself, emancipation, and the rhetoric of liberty weakened racism substantially and opened the window of opportunity so that the Fourteenth Amendment and Civil Rights laws were passed. Later on, by the

1870s, racism becomes a more prominent feature again. It returns in conjunction with views like social Darwinism and views of an innate hierarchy of intelligence and talent in the world. By the 1890s, racism was reinvigorated by hostility to immigration. So, I think we ought to look at the period of the Civil War and Reconstruction as a moment which illustrates that racism like all other things is a changeable phenomenon—it has ups and downs—and try to understand why this moment did occur.

Question: How has the Fourteenth Amendment been applied to the Bill of Rights under the doctrine of incorporation?

Answer: Under the doctrine of incorporation, the Fourteenth Amendment, through the "equal protection" clause, has applied nearly all of the Bill of Rights to the states as well as to the federal government. Incorporation developed in the twentieth century, beginning in the 1920s and then accelerated in the 1960s under the Warren Court. By now, most of the Bill of Rights have been incorporated to the states in a series of Supreme Court decisions. There is good evidence that the original intent of many of the framers of the Fourteenth Amendment, in particular Congressmen John Bingham of Ohio and Senator Jacob Howard of Michigan, was that at least the first eight amendments should be applied to the states. The problem with figuring out if that was the original intent or not is that the Fourteenth Amendment went through so many drafts and so many votes—there were seven to eight votes in the committee on Reconstruction which drafted the amendment—no single person or group actually was responsible. It was a compromise, and like all compromises there was a great deal that some people liked and some people did not like. But I do think the purpose of the Fourteenth Amendment was to empower the federal government to override the states if necessary to protect the rights of citizens. The doctrine of incorporation is an outgrowth of that purpose of the Fourteenth Amendment.

Suggestions for further reading:

Amar, Akhil Reed. *The Bill of Rights: Creation and Reconstruction*. New Haven: Yale University Press, 1998.

Belz, Herman. *A New Birth of Freedom: The Republican Party and Freedmen's Rights, 1861-1866*. New York: Fordham University Press, 2000.

Donald, David Herbert. *Lincoln*. New York: Simon and Schuster, 1995.

Foner, Eric. *Free Soil, Free Labor, Free Men: The Ideology of the Republican Party Before the Civil War*. New York: Oxford University Press, 1995.

_____. *The Story of American Freedom*. New York: W. W. Norton, 1998.

_____. *Reconstruction: America's Unfinished Revolution, 1863-1877*. New York: Harper and Row, 1988

Foner, Philip S. and George Walker. *Proceedings of the Black State Conventions, 1840-1865*, 2 vols. Philadelphia: Temple University Press, 1996.

Frederickson, George M. *The Inner Civil War: Northern Intellectuals and the Crisis of the Union*. Champaign-Urbana: University of Illinois Press, 1993.

Hess, Earl J. *Liberty, Virtue, and Progress: Northerners and Their War for the Union*. New York: Fordham University Press, 1997.

Hildebrand, Reginald F. *The Times Were Strange and Stirring: Methodist Preachers and the Crisis of Emancipation*. Durham: Duke University Press, 1995.

King, Richard H. *Civil Rights and the Idea of Freedom*. Athens: University of Georgia Press, 1996.

Nagel, Paul C. *The Sacred Trust: American Nationality 1798-1898*. New York: Oxford University Press, 1971.

Neely, Mark E. *The Fate of Liberty: Abraham Lincoln and Civil Liberties*. New York: Oxford University Press, 1991.

Robertson, James O. *American Myth, American Reality*. New York: Hill and Wang, 1982.

Rawls, John. *Political Liberalism*. New York: Columbia University Press, 1995.

Sundquist, Eric J. *To Wake the Nations: Race in the Making of American Literature*. Cambridge: Harvard University Press, 1993.

ABOUT THE CONTRIBUTORS

Ira Berlin—Distinguished University Professor, University of Maryland—College Park. Among his books are *Many Thousands Gone: The First Two Centuries of Slavery in Mainland North America* and *Slaves Without Masters: The Free Negro in the Antebellum South.* He also directed the *Freedom and Southern Society Project,* including the publication of the multi-volume *Freedom: A Documentary History of Emancipation* series.

David W. Blight—Class of 1959 Professor of History and Black Studies, Amherst College. Among his books are *Frederick Douglass's Civil War: Keeping the Faith in Jubilee* and *When This Cruel War is Over: The Civil War Letters of Charles Harvey Brewster,* which he edited. He is also the author of the upcoming *Race and Reunion: The Civil War in American Memory, 1863-1915.*

Drew Gilpin Faust—Dean, Radcliffe Institute for Advanced Study and Professor of History, Harvard University. Among her books are *Mothers of Invention: Women of the Slaveholding South in the American Civil War, The Creation of Confederate Nationalism: Ideology and Identity in the Civil War South,* and *James Henry Hammond and the Old South: A Design for Mastery.*

Eric Foner—Dewitt Clinton Professor of History, Columbia University. Among his books are *The Story of American Freedom; Reconstruction: America's Unfinished Revolution: 1863-1877; Politics and Ideology in the Age of the Civil War;* and *Free Soil, Free Labor, Free Men: Ideology of the Republican Party Before the Civil War.*

James Oliver Horton—Benjamin Banneker Professor of History, The George Washington University. Among his books are *Free People of Color: Inside the African American Community* and *The History of the African American People.* He co-authored with his wife, Lois E. Horton, *Community Among Free Blacks, 1700-1860.*

Jesse Jackson, Jr.—Member, United States House of Representatives, 2nd District, Illinois. He is the author of the upcoming book *A More Perfect Union.* Along with Jesse Jackson, Sr., he co-authored *It's About the Money: The Fourth Movement of the Freedom Symphony.*

Edward T. Linenthal—Edward M. Penson Professor of Religion and American Culture, University of Wisconsin, Oshkosh. Among his books are *Symbolic Defense: The Cultural Significance of the Strategic Defense Initiative; Sacred Ground: Americans and Their Battlefields,* and *Preserving Memory: The Struggle to Create America's Holocaust Museum.*

James M. McPherson—George Henry Davis '86 Professor of American History, Princeton University. Among his books are *Battle Cry of Freedom: The Civil War Era; Abraham Lincoln and the Second American Revolution; Drawn By the Sword: Reflections on the American Civil War* and *For Cause and Comrade: Why Men Fought in the Civil War.*

Robert K. Sutton—Superintendent, Manassas National Battlefield Park. Among his books are *Americans Interpret the Parthenon: The Progression of Greek Revival Architecture from the East Coast to Oregon, 1800-1860* and *Majestic in His Wrath: A Pictorial Life of Frederick Douglass,* for which he wrote the introduction.